Copyright © 2025 Juliana Makapan
First Edition

Published by Juliana Makapan
Self-Published in South Africa

ISBN (Print): 978-0-7961-7767-4
ISBN (eBook): 978-0-7961-7768-1

All rights reserved. No part of this book may be reproduced, stored, or transmitted in any form or by any means, electronic or mechanical, including photocopying, recording, or by any information storage and retrieval system, without the prior written permission of the author, except in the case of brief quotations embodied in critical articles and reviews.

Credits: Layout and design by Natasha Ungerer at DesignerArt

For permissions, inquiries, or more information, please contact:
julianam@telkomsa.net

Dedication

To God Almighty,

I dedicate these words to You in reverence, humility, and profound gratitude for the boundless wisdom and unwavering guidance illuminating every page of this book. Your divine inspiration has been the cornerstone of every thought, every sentence, and every revelation within these chapters.

In loving memory of my late parents, Obed and Eva Makapan whose nurturing embrace cultivated a passion for reading and writing in me. Their legacy lives on through these pages, a testament to their enduring influence.

To my children and grandchildren, whose unyielding support and boundless curiosity have been my greatest inspiration. Your voices echo through these words, shaping them with hope and purpose for future generations.

And to the courageous youth who tirelessly champion justice and equality in their communities, you are the heartbeat of change. May this book encourage your voices and fuel your dreams of a brighter tomorrow.

Welcome to the Journey

Prepare to embark on an epic adventure through the vibrant world of diversity, equity, inclusion and belonging! This book is your passport to a journey filled with mind-blowing discoveries, and some serious things to consider.

Imagine a world where every voice is not just heard but cherished. A world where our differences are not barriers, but beautiful threads that weave together the fabric of our communities. This book is your invitation to explore that world.

Each chapter is a step into a world where every voice is heard, every background is valued, and everyone is embraced for who they are. As you read, may you be inspired to see the world through new eyes, embrace differences with curiosity and compassion, and champion fairness and equality in our communities.

Together, let us embark on this enlightening adventure, where the colours of diversity paint a brighter, more inclusive future for everyone.

We invite you to open your hearts and minds as you journey through these pages. Let these lessons inspire you to embrace the differences that make us unique and to stand up for fairness and equity.

Together, we can create a world where everyone feels valued, respected, and included. So, come along and join us on this adventure of learning, understanding, and acceptance. The world is waiting and more beautiful when we are all included.

This is your chance to be a changemaker, a champion for kindness, and a builder of a better tomorrow.

So, are you ready to unfold your colours? Let us begin our journey together!

Contents

Chapter 1
Beginning Our Journey

Chapter 2
Understanding Diversity

Chapter 3
Equity in Action

Chapter 4
Inclusion

Chapter 5
Creating a Sense of Belonging

Chapter 6
Stereotypes and Bias

Chapter 7
You Are Unique

Chapter 8
Our Connected World

Chapter 9
Looking Towards the Future

Chapter 10
Advocacy and Social Justice

Chapter 11
Building Strong and Inclusive Communities

Chapter 12
A Call to Leaders of Tomorrow

Chapter 13
Power of Networking

Chapter 14
Inspiration in Action

Chapter 15
Together we Rise

Chapter 1
Beginning our Journey

"The Invisible Threads: Communities and Culture Shaping Who We Are"

Imagine a tree with roots, strong, hidden, and anchored to the ground, while its branches reach out towards the sun. These hidden roots represent communities and culture, the invisible forces that shape who we are, just like the roots shape the growth and direction of the tree.

Communities and culture play a significant role in shaping who we are as individuals, particularly during our Youth. The people we surround ourselves with and the environment we grow up in can have a profound impact on our values, beliefs, and behaviour.

Communities provide a sense of belonging and support that can be crucial for young people. Being a part of a community can help you develop a keen sense of identity and self-worth. Community involvement can also provide opportunities for Youth to gain leadership skills and other valuable experiences that can help them succeed.

Culture is another crucial factor in shaping who we are. Cultural traditions, beliefs, and values can influence our worldview and how we interact with others. Exposure to diverse cultures can broaden our perspectives and help us develop empathy and understanding for others.

For young people, experiencing diverse cultures can be particularly transformative. It can help develop a respect for diversity and challenge any biases or prejudices you may have. Cultural exchange programs, travel, and exposure to diverse communities can all help Youth broaden their horizons and develop a more open-minded and inclusive outlook.

In short, the communities we belong to and the cultures we experience can have a profound impact on who we are as individuals. Youth who are exposed to diverse communities and cultures can develop a powerful sense of identity, empathy, and respect for others, which can help them become successful and engaged members of society.

What is a community?

Community refers to a group of people who share common interests, values, and goals, and who live in the same area or geographical location. Communities can be formed based on numerous factors, such as ethnicity, religion, culture, or shared experiences.

Being part of a community provides a sense of belonging and support and allows individuals to work together towards common goals and overcome challenges.

Examples of communities

Communities can be formed based on numerous factors such as:

Geographical location: People living in the same neighbourhood, city, or region often form communities united by their geographic proximity and shared experiences.

- Example

Rural Towns: In small rural towns, residents often know each other and come together for community events like town fairs, parades, and local sports games. These towns usually have strong community bonds due to their smaller size and shared way of life.

Ethnicity or race: People who share the same ethnic or racial background often form communities that celebrate their shared heritage, culture, and history.

- Example

Jewish communities: Jewish communities, both in Israel and the diaspora, come together to celebrate religious and cultural events like Hanukkah, Passover, and Purim. These communities often have strong social networks through synagogues, cultural centers, and schools.

Religion: People who share the same religious beliefs often form tight-knit communities supporting each other and practicing their faith together.

- *Example*

Church congregations: In many Christian denominations, church members gather weekly for worship services, Bible studies, and community events. These congregations often support each other through life's challenges and celebrations.

Language: People who speak the same language often form communities to share their culture, support each other, and maintain their linguistic heritage.

- *Example*

Portuguese-speaking communities: Portuguese-speaking communities, particularly those from Brazil and Portugal, are found in various parts of the world. These communities often come together to celebrate cultural events, maintain Portuguese-language schools, and support each other through community organisations.

Shared interests: People who share common interests, such as sports, music, or hobbies, often form communities where they can connect, share their passion, and support each other.

Outdoor adventure groups

- *Examples*

Hiking clubs: Nature lovers join hiking clubs to explore trails, share outdoor experiences, and promote environmental conservation.

CrossFit gyms: Members of CrossFit gyms participate in high-intensity workouts, challenge each other, and celebrate fitness achievements.

Writers' groups: Aspiring and established writers join groups to share their work, receive feedback, and support each other's writing journeys

Profession

People who work in the same profession or industry often form communities to share knowledge, network, and support each other's career growth.

- *Examples*

Hospital staff: Doctors, nurses, and other healthcare workers collaborate in hospitals, sharing knowledge and working together to provide patient care.

School faculty: Teachers and administrators within a school work together to educate students, share teaching strategies, and support each other.

Law firms: Lawyers, paralegals, and support staff within a law firm collaborate on cases, share legal knowledge, and provide mutual support.

Shared experiences

People who have gone through similar experiences often form communities to provide support, share insights, and foster a sense of belonging.

-Examples

Support groups: Cancer survivors often join support groups where they can share their journeys, offer encouragement, and discuss coping strategies. Organisations like the American Cancer Society facilitate these groups.

Parenting groups: New parents often join local or online parenting groups to share advice, discuss challenges, and support each other. Groups like MOPS (Mothers of Preschoolers) and local mom/dad groups are common.

Online grief support communities: Websites like Grieving.com and online forums provide spaces for individuals to discuss their grief, share memories, and support each other through the healing process.

These are just a few examples of the many diverse types of communities that provide a sense of belonging and support, allowing individuals to work together towards common goals and overcome challenges.

Here are some additional examples of communities that relate to Youth:

School communities: Students who attend the same school can form a community based on shared experiences, interests, and goals. Many schools have student councils or student governments where students can take on leadership roles and work together to improve their school environment.

Sports teams: Young athletes who are part of the same sports team can form a community based on shared interests and experiences. Community and school-based Youth soccer leagues offer young players the chance to develop their skills, compete, and build friendships.

Online communities: Youth who share common interests can connect and form communities through social media or other online platforms. Language learning app Duolingo has forums where young learners can discuss language learning tips, share progress, and practice together.

Youth groups: Youth organisations such as Scouts, 4-H, or religious groups can provide a sense of community and belonging for young people. The YMCA offers a variety of Youth programs including sports, leadership training, and camps, aimed at fostering personal growth and community involvement.

Cultural communities: Youth who share the same cultural background can form a community based on shared traditions, values, and beliefs. Cultural centers often have dance troupes for Youth to learn traditional dances, perform at events, and connect with their cultural heritage.

Volunteer organisations: Youth who volunteer together for a common cause can form a community based on shared interests and goals. Programs that engage young people in building homes and participating in community service projects.

These examples illustrate the diverse ways in which Youth can participate in and benefit from various communities and organisations, fostering their growth, skills, and sense of belonging.

Being part of a community provides a sense of belonging and support and allows Youth to work together towards common goals and overcome challenges. These communities can help young people develop important life skills such as teamwork, leadership, and communication.

What is culture?

Imagine your family has a special recipe for grandma's famous cookies. This recipe, along with the way you celebrate birthdays or how you greet each other, are all part of your culture. Culture is like a unique language shared by a group of people. It is everything that makes us special.

The collection of customs, traditions, language, art, music, food, and shared values that define a group of people. It is how we celebrate holidays, the stories we tell, the clothes we wear, the languages we speak, and the way we interact with each other. Culture shapes our identity and helps us understand where we come from, who we are, and how we connect with others.

Culture is like a big, colourful quilt made up of many different patches. Each patch represents a different part of who we are and where we come from. Let us look at some of these patches:

Food is a big part of culture! It is not just about what we eat, but how we prepare it, when we eat it, and even who we eat it with. For example, in Japan, there is a special ceremony called a "tea ceremony," in which they creatively prepare and serve matcha green tea. It is not just about drinking tea; it is about appreciating the moment and the company.

Enjoying cultural dishes like tacos, sushi, curry, or pasta, and learning to cook family recipes.

Language is not just about words; it is about how we communicate and express ourselves. For example, in many African cultures, storytelling is a big part of passing down traditions and history. The way stories are told, the language used, the dialects, and the gestures all play a part in preserving and sharing culture.

The language(s) you speak at home or with friends, including slang and phrases unique to your group, are an important part of your culture.

Music is like a universal language that can convey emotions and stories. Diverse cultures have their unique styles and instruments. For example, in African cultures, drums are often used not just for music but also for communication. The rhythms and beats can carry messages across long distances, even to animals.

The music you listen to, the dances you perform, the art you create, and the stories you enjoy all contribute to your cultural identity.

Celebrations are a time to come together and rejoice in our shared culture. Diverse cultures have different celebrations for several reasons. For example, in Mexico, Independence Day is celebrated on September 16th, marked by parades, music, and fireworks. Traditional dances like the Jarabe Tapatío (Mexican Hat Dance) and regional cuisines also play significant roles in Mexican culture.

Think about the holidays you celebrate with your family, the special meals you have, and the rituals or ceremonies you participate in. These are all part of your culture.

Beliefs are like the foundation of culture, shaping how we see the world and our place in it. The Māori culture of New Zealand has a belief in "whakapapa," which refers to genealogy and the idea that all things are interconnected through ancestry. Whakapapa is not just about tracing lineage but also understanding the relationships between all living things and the land. It emphasizes respect for ancestors, the environment, and the interconnectedness of past, present, and future generations. This belief is central to Māori identity and influences their relationships, customs, and traditions.

The ***values*** your family and community uphold, like respect, honesty, and kindness, and the beliefs you share, whether religious, spiritual, or philosophical, are core aspects of your culture.

Clothing can be a powerful expression of culture, representing traditions, values, and identity. The kimono in Japan is not just a piece of clothing but a symbol of cultural pride and heritage. Clothing often reflects a person's identity, including their culture, values, and beliefs. It can express individuality or group affiliation, such as cultural heritage or social status.

The styles, types, and traditions of clothing we wear, including traditional outfits, are for special occasions, everyday wear, and the influence of fashion trends within a community.

Arts and crafts preserve the heritage and traditions of a society, passing them down from generation to generation. They help maintain a sense of identity and continuity with the past. Overall, arts and crafts play a vital role in enriching society, promoting understanding between cultures, and contributing to the overall quality of life.

Creative expressions such as painting, drawing, sculpture, knitting, and crafting is unique to a culture. This includes traditional crafts passed down through generations as well as modern artistic expressions.

Architectural styles often reflect cultural values and beliefs. Architecture reflects the culture and identity of a society. It can be influenced by local traditions, materials, and building techniques, serving as a visual representation of a community's history and values.

Visiting historical buildings like castles, temples, and traditional houses, and appreciating the design of modern community centers or schools.

Family structure and values have a strong influence on individual growth and development. The way families are structured and the values they uphold can vary greatly between cultures. For example, in some cultures, extended family members play a significant role in raising children and making decisions.

The customs, routines, and traditions you have within your family, like weekly family dinners or movie nights, contribute to your family culture.

Education and knowledge are passed down from generation to generation and can be a unique aspect of culture. For example, in some Indigenous cultures, oral traditions are used to preserve history and teachings.

Attending language classes to learn a heritage language or participating in cultural studies courses.

Relationships and social interactions with each other can be influenced by cultural norms and values. For example, in some cultures, there are specific ways to show respect to elders or greet strangers.

Greeting elders with respect, participating in community festivals, and engaging in online forums or social media groups.

Sports and games can be a fun way to learn about a culture. For example, traditional Masai jumping dances in East Africa are not just for entertainment but also a way to display strength and agility.

Playing traditional sports like cricket, soccer, or basketball, and participating in community sports leagues.

These aspects, along with others, all contribute to the rich tapestry of culture that makes each community and society unique. Culture is incredibly diverse and multifaceted. Each of these aspects of culture is like a piece of a puzzle. When you put us all together, you get a beautiful picture of who we are and where we come from.

Understanding culture helps Youth appreciate their background and be open to learning about and respecting the cultures of others, fostering a more inclusive and connected world.

Let us explore with examples!

Traditions: France might celebrate Bastille Day with parades, while Mexico might have Day of the Dead celebrations.

Food: France is known for croissants and baguettes, while Mexico might have tacos and burritos.

Music and dance: France has the Can-can dance, while Mexico has traditional dances like the Jarabe Tapatío.

Language: French and Spanish are spoken in these countries, with unique sounds and phrases.

- Example

Let us create an example of a fictional sports team called the "Spirit Runners." They are a team of long-distance runners from a fictional country called Lumaria, known for it is vibrant culture. Here is how we can incorporate various aspects of culture into their story:

Clothing: The Spirit Runners wear traditional Lumarian running attire, which includes brightly coloured tunics and leggings, adorned with intricate patterns that represent various aspects of Lumarian life, such as nature, unity, and strength.

Music: Before each race, the Spirit Runners perform a traditional Lumarian drumming ceremony. The rhythmic beats of the drums not only pump up the team but also serve to connect with their cultural roots and invoke the spirit of their ancestors for strength and guidance.

Language: The team has a special chant in the Lumarian language that they recite before and after each race. The chant is a call for unity and perseverance, reminding us of the values that their culture holds dear.

Celebrations: After a successful race, the Spirit Runners celebrate with a feast that includes traditional Lumarian dishes, such as savoury stewed vegetables, hearty grains, and sweet pastries. The feast is a time for the team to bond and reflect on their accomplishments.

Beliefs: The Spirit Runners believe in the concept of "spirit running," which is more than just physical running. It is about connecting with the land, the spirit is, and each other. They believe that by running with purpose and intention, they can bring harmony to their community.

Arts and crafts: The team carries small tokens of art crafted by

Lumarian artisans. These tokens serve as reminders of their culture and heritage, and they believe that they bring luck and protection during races.

Family structure and values: Many of the Spirit Runners come from large, extended families, and their families play a significant role in their lives and their running careers. Family members often travel with the team to provide support and encouragement.

The Spirit Runners exemplify how sports can be deeply intertwined with culture, serving to celebrate traditions, express identity, and uphold values.

Making connections

Learning about diverse cultures is like learning unfamiliar words in a language. It helps us understand each other better, appreciate our differences, and celebrate the amazing diversity of our world.

So next time you try new food, listen to a different kind of music, or learn a new greeting in another language, remember that you are exploring the wonderful world of culture!

How do communities and culture shape us?

Communities and culture play a key role in shaping who we are as individuals. Communities provide a sense of belonging and support and influence our values, beliefs, and behaviours through shared experiences, norms, and traditions.

Culture, on the other hand, shapes the way we perceive the world, communicate with others, and express ourselves through art, music, language, and other forms of expression.

Growing up in a particular community and culture can influence our identity, worldview, and sense of belonging. For example, cultural traditions and values can instill a sense of pride and identity in individuals, while community norms and expectations can influence our behaviours and decisions.

Being exposed to different communities and cultures can broaden our perspectives and help us appreciate diversity. It is important to keep an open mind and embrace the richness of diverse cultures and communities.

Just like the roots of a tree silently nurture its growth, our communities and culture influence our behaviours, attitudes, and even values in several ways such as:

1. Identity

Sense of belonging: Culture provides a sense of belonging by connecting Youth to a shared history, traditions, and values. This fosters self-esteem and a positive identity.

Values and beliefs: Cultural practices and community norms shape young people's understanding of right and wrong, influencing their decision-making and moral compass.

2. Social development

Social skills: Communities offer opportunities to interact with peers, learn communication skills, and build healthy relationships, fostering cooperation, empathy, and respect.

Modelling and reinforcement: We observe and learn from the behaviour of others within our communities. We are more likely to adopt certain behaviours when praised and rewarded. Conversely, behaviours that are punished or ostracised become less likely.

3. Language and communication

Language development: Culture heavily influences the language Youth speak and the way we communicate. Dialects, slang, and specific greetings are often learned within communities.

Appreciation of diversity: Exposure to different languages and communication styles within diverse communities helps Youth to develop respect and understanding for different perspectives.

4. Knowledge and skills

Cultural knowledge: Young people learn about their heritage, traditions, and history through cultural practices and community events, fostering a sense of cultural pride and understanding.

Life skills: Communities can provide opportunities for Youth to learn valuable life skills like cooking, crafting, or playing music, which can contribute to their overall development.

5. Personal expression

Creative outlets: Culture and communities often provide platforms for artistic expression through music, dance, storytelling, or visual arts, allowing Youth to express themselves creatively and explore their individuality.

Cultural identity exploration: As Youth interact with diverse cultural influences within their communities, we can explore and define their own cultural identity, embracing their heritage while potentially incorporating aspects from diverse backgrounds.

6. Environmental factors

Resource availability: The resources available within a community can impact behaviour. Poverty, limited access to education, or a lack of opportunities can lead to increased crime, substance abuse, and other negative behaviours.

Physical environment: The design and layout of our communities can influence behaviour. Public spaces that are safe, well-maintained, and encourage interaction can foster positive social norms and community engagement. Conversely, neglected or unsafe environments can contribute to feelings of isolation and antisocial behaviour.

Drawbacks of cultural and community influences on Youth

While cultural and community influences can be incredibly positive, there are also potential drawbacks to consider:

1. Limited perspectives

Gender roles: In some cultures, rigid gender roles might limit the career or life choices for young people, particularly for girls who are expected to pursue specific professions or prioritise family duties.

Conformity pressure: Strong community expectations might pressure Youth to conform to specific norms, even if these do not resonate with their values or interests. This can stifle individuality and discourage exploring diverse perspectives.

2. Negative influences

Prejudice and discrimination: Cultural or community beliefs can sometimes lead to prejudice and discrimination against individuals or groups who differ in terms of religion, ethnicity, or other social identities. This can create a hostile environment for young people who belong to minority groups.

Harmful traditions: Certain deeply rooted cultural practices can be harmful, like female genital mutilation or child marriage. These traditions can negatively impact young people's physical and mental well-being and require critical thinking and external intervention in response.

3. Limited access to opportunities

Socioeconomic factors: Depending on the community, economic limitations might restrict access to quality education, healthcare, or extracurricular activities, hindering young people's opportunities for growth and development.

Cultural isolation: In some cases, strong cultural identities within communities can lead to social isolation from individuals from diverse backgrounds, limiting opportunities for diverse interactions and experiences.

Remember that these examples are not exhaustive, and the drawbacks can vary greatly depending on the specific culture and community. However, acknowledging these potential drawbacks allows for open discussions, critical thinking, and the development of strategies to mitigate negative influences while fostering the positive aspects of cultural and community belonging for young people.

It is essential to keep in mind that Youth also have a significant amount of power to shape our communities, even though it is undeniable that a community can affect individual behaviour.

We all have the option to choose how we behave, and what we do can ultimately contribute to the development of the kind of community in which we would like to live. We can make our communities stronger and more cohesive places to live when we collaborate on common objectives.

If they are aware of the positive and negative aspects of cultural and community influence, Youth can make informed decisions about their own beliefs and behaviours, and work towards building positive and inclusive communities.

How can we address the drawbacks of cultural and community influences?

We can create environments where culture and community influence, empower and support all Youth. This fosters a society that celebrates diversity, ensures equity of opportunity, promotes inclusion, and allows everyone to feel a keen sense of belonging.

Closing reflections

As we reach the end of this chapter on the profound impact of culture and communities on youth, let us take a moment to reflect on the incredible influence that our environments and traditions have on shaping who we are. Imagine a world where every young person is deeply rooted in a community that nurtures their growth, celebrates their culture, and supports their journey. This is the world we can create together.

Culture and communities are the bedrock of our identities. They provide us with a sense of belonging, a source of pride, and a foundation of values and traditions. For youth, being part of a supportive community and understanding their cultural heritage is essential for their personal development and sense of self.

Think of culture as the rich soil that nourishes a young plant. It offers the nutrients, stability, and support needed for the plant to grow strong and resilient. Similarly, a vibrant community acts as the garden where this growth occurs, providing a safe space for youth to explore, learn, and thrive. Together, culture and community shape the future by investing in the growth and potential of the next generation.

However, the journey towards embracing and understanding one's culture and community is not always straightforward. Youth may face challenges such as cultural misunderstandings, societal pressures, or a lack of representation. It requires courage to stand firm in one's cultural identity and to seek out communities that support and uplift. But every step taken towards cultural appreciation and community building strengthens the individual and enriches society.

In celebrating culture and fostering strong communities, we do not just change the world—we transform it. We create a world where every young person can discover their roots, embrace their heritage, and contribute to a community that supports their dreams. This is the legacy we leave for the next generation—a legacy of unity, pride, and endless possibilities.

Call to Action

Let us commit to being agents of cultural appreciation and community builders. Every act of engagement, no matter how small, has the power to create ripples of positive change. Let us start today and let us do it together.

Encourage others to see the beauty in diverse cultures and the strength in united communities. Together, we can build a future where every young person feels connected, valued, and inspired.

Thought to Ponder

How can you, in your daily life, honor your culture and contribute to a community that supports and uplifts every young person?

As you move forward, carry with you the belief that culture and community are powerful forces that shape our lives. Be a champion for cultural understanding and community engagement in your schools, neighbourhoods, and beyond.

By embracing culture and community, you hold the key to unlocking a world where every individual is celebrated, every tradition is honored, and every community is strong. Let us make this vision a reality, one step at a time.

Let us move our journey to Diversity, Equity, Inclusion *and Belonging.*

Chapter 2
Understanding Diversity

"Different Vibes, Stronger Tribes: Embrace the Power of Diverse Perspectives."

What is diversity?

Diversity has various definitions and thus cannot be easily defined.

It is like a rainbow: Every colour is unique and beautiful, but together they create something even more amazing.

Think pizza: You would not want just one topping, right? Diversity is like having all the different ingredients and delicious flavours together, making the pizza even better.

It is like an orchestra: Each instrument has its sound, but when they play together, they create beautiful music.

The following are some of the simple definitions of diversity that we can use in this book:

"Diversity is differences among people concerning age, class, ethnicity, gender, physical and mental ability, race, sexual orientation, spiritual practice, and other human differences." – Kathy Castania

"Diversity means understanding that everyone is unique and recognising our differences. These can be along the dimensions of race, ethnicity, gender, sexual orientation, socio-economic status, age, physical abilities, religious beliefs, political beliefs, or other ideologies." – Office of Equity and Inclusion Oregon Health Authority

Diversity as used here in this sentence refers to human attributes that are different from your own and from those of groups to which you belong." – The University of Michigan

Diversity, in a practical sense, is all about the differences that make each person unique. It is like a big, colourful puzzle where every piece is different and important. When we talk about diversity, we are talking about all the things that make us who we are.

Key elements of diversity

1. Gender: This refers to the socially constructed roles, behaviours, activities, and attributes that a society considers appropriate for men, women, and other gender identities.

Gender diversity includes recognising and respecting different gender identities, expressions, and experiences and promoting gender equality and respect for all.

2. Age: Diversity acknowledges and values the perspectives, experiences, and contributions of individuals across different life stages, from youth to older adults.

It recognises the unique perspectives and strengths that people of different ages bring to a community or organisation.

3. Race and ethnicity: Race refers to a social construct that categorizes individuals based on physical characteristics, while ethnicity refers to cultural traditions, ancestry, and a shared sense of identity.

Racial and ethnic diversity encompasses the recognition and appreciation of different racial and ethnic backgrounds, including their unique histories, traditions, and perspectives.

4. Culture: Culture encompasses the values, beliefs, customs, languages, and practices that shape individuals' and groups' ways of life.

Cultural diversity recognises and respects the various cultural backgrounds, traditions, and perspectives that coexist within a society or organisation.

5. Sexual orientation: Sexual orientation refers to an individual's romantic, emotional, and sexual attraction to others.

Sexual orientation includes recognizing and respecting individuals who identify as heterosexual, gay, lesbian, bisexual, asexual, or any other sexual orientation.

6. Religion and spiritual beliefs: Religion and spiritual beliefs encompass the diverse systems of faith, practices, and beliefs that individuals and communities hold.

Diversity in this area involves respecting and accommodating different religious and spiritual traditions, as well as individuals who do not subscribe to any religion.

7. Disability: Diversity recognises and values individuals with physical, cognitive, sensory, or other disabilities.

It involves creating inclusive environments that accommodate and empower individuals with diverse abilities and ensuring equal opportunities and access.

8. Socioeconomic status: Socioeconomic diversity recognises and values individuals from different economic backgrounds, levels of education, and social classes.

It involves creating opportunities and removing barriers for individuals from diverse socioeconomic circumstances.

9. Family structure: Family structures can vary greatly, including single parents, blended families, multigenerational households, same-sex parents, and other non-traditional family arrangements.

Recognising and respecting diverse family structures is an important aspect of diversity.

10. Educational background and cognitive diversity: Individuals come from diverse educational backgrounds, including varying levels of formal education, fields of study, and types of institutions attended.

Additionally, cognitive diversity encompasses diverse ways of thinking, problem-solving styles, and perspectives, which can contribute to a more comprehensive understanding of issues.

11. Geographic location and regional diversity: An individual's geographic location and regional background can shape their experiences, perspectives, and cultural influences.

This includes differences between urban, suburban, and rural areas, as well as variations across regions, states, or countries.

12. *Language and communication styles:* Language diversity encompasses the recognition and inclusion of individuals who speak different languages, dialects, or communication styles. This can include accommodating individuals who use sign language, have different accents, or communicate in unique ways.

13. *Life experiences and personal backgrounds:* Everyone has a unique set of life experiences, personal backgrounds, and circumstances that shape their perspectives and worldviews.

This can include experiences related to immigration, military service, trauma, or other significant life events.

These are just some of the key elements of diversity. Embracing diversity means recognising, respecting, and valuing the unique characteristics, perspectives, and experiences that individuals and groups bring to a community or organisation.

Promoting diversity fosters inclusivity, understanding, and the exchange of diverse ideas and perspectives, which can lead to innovation, creativity, and personal growth.

These elements of diversity come together to make each person unique. When we embrace diversity, we celebrate these differences and recognise the value that each person brings to our communities and our world.

Consequences of a lack of diversity awareness

A lack of diversity awareness in a young person's life can have far-reaching and damaging consequences. Here is a breakdown of some key negative impacts:

1. Limited worldview and distorted perceptions

Misinformed understanding of others: Without exposure to diverse cultures, races, abilities, and backgrounds, Youth may develop skewed or inaccurate assumptions about people who are different from them. This can lead to prejudice and discrimination.

Reinforces "us vs. them" mentality: Homogeneous environments breed a sense of isolation and can create a narrow "in-group" mentality that fosters fear or resentment of the "other."

Lack of empathy: Young people need diverse social interactions to learn how to see the world from different perspectives, developing crucial empathy that helps build healthy relationships.

Prejudice and discrimination: When we are not exposed to diversity, we are more likely to develop biases and stereotypes about people who are different from us. This can lead to harmful behaviours later in life.

2. Psychological impacts and self-esteem

Feeling invisible or excluded: If a young person does not encounter people who share their background or identity, they may feel isolated and invisible, contributing to feelings of self-doubt or marginalisation.

Internalised negative stereotypes: When media, education, and social circles lack representation, a young person may internalise negative stereotypes about their group, damaging their self-esteem and sense of belonging.

Pressure to conform: In a non-diverse environment, there is often pressure for those who are different to downplay their identity and conform to the dominant norm, leading to self-suppression.

Stagnant thinking: Without a diversity of ideas, groups can fall into echo chambers where everyone thinks alike. This reduces innovation and problem-solving abilities.

3. Missed opportunities for development and growth

Limited critical thinking skills: Diverse groups are better at tackling complex problems due to the variety of perspectives they bring. Kids in less diverse environments miss this valuable skill-building.

Less preparation for a diverse world: Today's world is highly interconnected. Young people need to develop cultural competency and the ability to navigate diverse settings to thrive in careers and society.

Missed friendships and connections: Diverse friendships enrich lives and broaden horizons. Lacking such exposure limits potential connections and experiences for young people.

Missed opportunities: We miss the chance to learn about diverse cultures, perspectives, and ways of thinking. This limit is our worldview and creativity in problem-solving.

Why is diversity important for Youth?

Diversity is particularly important to Youth because it helps shape their perspectives, values, and ability to navigate an increasingly diverse world. Here are some key reasons why diversity is crucial at the Youth level:

1. Development of empathy and understanding

Exposure to diversity from a youthful age helps children and adolescents develop empathy, understanding, and respect for diverse cultures, backgrounds, and identities.

This awareness can foster more inclusive and tolerant attitudes, reducing prejudice and discrimination.

2. Preparation for a diverse workforce and society

Today's Youth will enter a workforce and society that is increasingly diverse. By experiencing diversity early on, young people can develop the necessary skills and mindsets to effectively communicate, collaborate, and interact with individuals from various backgrounds.

In a globally connected world, understanding and respecting diversity prepares youth to interact positively and effectively in international settings.

3. Fostering creativity and critical thinking

Diverse classrooms and Youth environments encourage the exchange of diverse ideas, perspectives, and experiences.

This exposure can enhance creativity, critical thinking, and problem-solving abilities, as young minds are challenged to consider different viewpoints and approaches.

4. Representation and role models

Diversity among peers, educators, and role models provides Youth from underrepresented or marginalised groups with positive examples to aspire to. This representation can boost self-confidence, motivation, and a sense of belonging.

5. Appreciation of cultural richness

Celebrating diversity in Youth settings, such as through cultural events, curricula, or extracurricular activities, can foster an appreciation of the richness of diverse cultures, traditions, and experiences.

This can broaden young people's horizons and promote intercultural understanding.

6. Prevention of biases and stereotypes

By exposing Youth to diversity early on, there is an opportunity to address and prevent the development of biases, stereotypes, and prejudices that can form due to lack of exposure or limited perspectives.

Exposure to diverse groups promotes a more just and equitable society.

7. Promotion of social justice and equity

Embracing diversity in Youth settings can help raise awareness about issues of social justice, equity, and inclusivity. This awareness can empower young people to become advocates for positive change and work towards creating more equitable and just communities.

Understanding diversity encourages youth to advocate for equity and inclusion, ensuring that all individuals have equal opportunities and support.

By prioritising diversity at the Youth level, we can help shape future generations that are more open-minded, culturally aware, and better equipped to navigate and contribute to an increasingly diverse and interconnected world.

Barriers to promoting diversity

Lack of awareness. Without learning about diverse cultures and backgrounds, young people might not understand why diversity is important. For example, in some schools, there might be limited or no teaching about the history and contributions of diverse cultures.

Limited understanding or knowledge about diverse cultures, backgrounds, and experiences can create resistance to diversity initiatives.

Prejudice and stereotyping. When young people hold biased views or stereotypes about others, it can lead to discrimination and exclusion. For instance, if a group of friends believes that people from a certain background are "dangerous," they might avoid befriending someone from that background.

Preconceived notions and biases about certain groups can hinder the acceptance and inclusion of diverse individuals.

Social pressure. Sometimes, young people feel pressured by their friends or community to act or think in a certain way. This pressure can make it hard for them to embrace diversity. For example, a teenager might hesitate to speak up for a friend who is being bullied because they fear being excluded from their social group.

Peer pressure and societal expectations can discourage individuals from supporting diversity initiatives or engaging with people from diverse backgrounds.

Limited access to resources. In some communities, there may be a lack of resources that promote diversity, such as diverse books, movies, or community events. Without access to these resources, young people may not have the opportunity to gain experience about and appreciate diverse cultures. For example, a neighbourhood might not have a library that offers books in different languages or about diverse cultures.

Lack of access to resources such as education, funding, and support programs can prevent marginalised groups from fully participating in diverse environments.

Fear of the unknown. Meeting people from diverse backgrounds can be intimidating if you are not familiar with their culture or customs. For instance, a young person might feel nervous about attending a cultural festival because they are not sure what to expect.

Fear of unfamiliar cultures, practices, and perspectives can create resistance to embracing diversity and inclusivity.

Lack of representation. When young people do not see people who look like them in leadership positions or media, they might feel like they do not belong or that their voice is not important. For example, if all the main characters in a TV show are from the same background, it can send the message that only people from that background are important or valued.

The absence of diverse role models and leaders can make it difficult to promote diversity and inspire inclusive practices.

Language and communication barriers. Differences in language and communication styles can make it hard for young people from diverse backgrounds to understand each other. For example, if a group of friends includes someone who speaks a different language at home, they might struggle to communicate effectively with that person.

Differences in language can create communication challenges and misunderstandings, making it difficult to foster inclusive interactions.

Systemic inequality. In some communities, there are systemic barriers that make it harder for young people from diverse backgrounds to succeed. For example, if a school district allocates more resources to schools in wealthier neighbourhoods, students from lower-income or marginalised communities might not have access to the same opportunities.

Systemic discrimination and unequal opportunities based on race, gender, sexuality, or other factors can impede efforts to create diverse environments.

Cultural insensitivity. Sometimes, young people might not realise that their actions or words are hurtful to others. For example, making jokes about someone's culture or traditions can be insensitive and create barriers to building positive relationships.

Traditions and cultural norms that prioritise homogeneity can resist changes that promote diversity and inclusion.

Addressing these barriers requires a commitment to education, empathy, and inclusivity from individuals, communities, and institutions. By promoting understanding and celebrating differences, we can create a more inclusive and diverse society for all young people.

Opportunities that diversity offers

Living in a diverse society allows you to constantly learn about new cultures, perspectives, and ways of life. Having friends, classmates, and colleagues from different racial, ethnic, or national backgrounds expands your horizons.

You gain new insights into how people from other cultures view the world. You pick up an appreciation of different foods, styles of dress, languages, traditions, and art forms. This cross-cultural pollination sparks creativity and innovation. Scientists have found that diverse teams outperform homogeneous ones at problem-solving by considering more perspectives.

Immersing yourself in diversity from a youthful age also makes you comfortable being around all types of people. An open and curious mindset about people's differences becomes second nature. You develop the critical skills of cross-cultural communication and emotional intelligence. These competencies will be vitally important for work and life in our globalised society and economy.

Furthermore, standing up for and celebrating diversity is the ethical path towards a more just, equitable world. By rejecting prejudices, questioning assumptions, and forming authentic connections across groups, you can be part of the solution to reducing discrimination, hatred, and conflict.

Each diverse encounter is an opportunity to further the human family's understanding of one another.

Challenges of diversity

Despite the tremendous opportunities diversity presents, its navigation brings difficult challenges, especially for Youth. You will likely encounter covert or overt prejudices, stereotyping, and discrimination at some point based on your race, religion, gender, sexual orientation, or other aspects of your identity.

Racial divisions, culture clashes, miscommunications, and conflicts arising from diversity are still realities in schools, neighbourhoods, and workplaces.

The prejudices you face may come from peers, teachers, community members, institutions, or larger social narratives and portrayals. These prejudices can profoundly impact your self-esteem, feelings of belonging, opportunities, and overall well-being.

You may experience alienation, loneliness, anxiety, depression, or anger. Witnessing or experiencing discrimination or hate can be frightening and psychologically damaging.

The pressures of navigating multiple cultures and identities can also create profound internal conflicts and identity struggles. You may feel torn between trying to assimilate or preserve your authentic heritage and roots.

Adopting certain practices of the mainstream culture may lead to accusations of disloyalty or counterfeiting from members of your home community. The cumulative stresses of dealing with biases and culture clashes can take an emotional, mental, and physical toll.

Closing reflections

Diversity is not just about acknowledging our differences—it is about celebrating them. It is about recognising that each one of us brings something special to the table, whether it is a unique perspective, a new idea, or a unique way of solving problems. By embracing diversity, we unlock a world of possibilities, enriching our lives and communities in ways we never thought possible.

Think about the strongest trees in a forest. They are not all the same; they are different in height, shape, and species. Yet, their diversity makes the forest resilient, vibrant, and full of life. Similarly, our diversity makes us stronger, more creative, and more connected. When we stand together, embracing our differences, we become a powerful force for change.

As you move forward, carry with you the belief that diversity is our greatest strength. Be a champion for inclusion in your schools, communities, and beyond. Encourage others to see the beauty in our differences and to value the contributions of every individual. Together, we can build a future where everyone feels seen, heard, and valued.

In embracing diversity, we do not just change the world—we transform it. We create a world where everyone can thrive, where innovation flourishes, and where compassion reigns. This is the legacy we leave for the next generation, a legacy of unity, strength, and boundless possibilities.

So, let us step into this future with open hearts and minds, ready to embrace the incredible diversity that makes our world so wonderfully unique. The journey ahead is filled with challenges, but also with immense rewards. Together, we can have influence. Together, we can build a better, more inclusive world.

Call to Action

Let us commit to being agents of change, champions of diversity, and builders of a brighter future. Every act of inclusion, no matter how small, has the power to transform our world. Let us start today and let us do it together.

Thought to Ponder

How can you, in your daily life, be a beacon of diversity and inclusion, inspiring others to see the world through a lens of acceptance and love?

By embracing diversity, you hold the key to unlocking a world where every person is celebrated, every voice is heard, and every dream is possible. Let us make this vision a reality, one step at a time.

"This is the world we can create together."

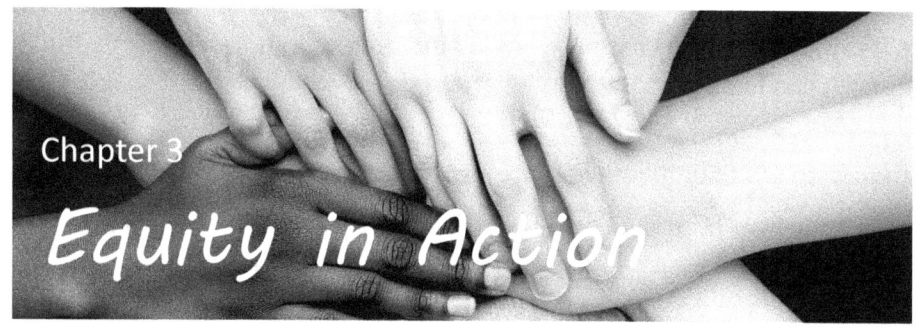

Chapter 3
Equity in Action

"Equal Rights, Equal Fights: Stand Up for Equity, Everywhere!"
What is equity?

Equity refers to the practice of ensuring that all individuals have access to the resources, opportunities, and support they need to achieve their full potential, regardless of their background, identity, or circumstances.

Equity recognises that individuals may face different barriers and challenges based on their unique experiences and identities, it seeks to address these disparities by providing targeted support and resources.

Equity is different from equality, which refers to the idea of treating everyone the same. While equality can be an important principle, it does not consider how different individuals may have unique needs and experiences.

Equity, on the other hand, recognises that individuals may require various levels of support and resources to achieve equitable outcomes.

A student with a disability may require additional accommodations or support to achieve the same level of academic success as their non-disabled peers. Providing this additional support and resources is an example of equity in action.

Equity can involve a range of strategies and approaches, including targeted outreach, resource allocation, and policy changes. By promoting equity, we can work towards creating more just and equitable societies where all individuals can thrive and reach their full potential.

- *Imagine a seesaw:* Everyone deserves to be on the same level, even if their starting points are different. That is equity!

- ***It is like sharing a cake:*** Everyone gets a slice, so nobody feels left out. That is fair and equitable!
- ***It is like playing a game:*** Everyone gets the same rules and the same chance to win. Equity makes sure everyone is on equal footing.

Equity, for Youth, means ensuring that everyone has what they need to succeed, regardless of their background or circumstances. It is about fairness and giving each person the support and resources they need to reach their full potential.

Imagine a race where everyone is given a pair of shoes to wear. Equity would mean that each person gets a pair of shoes that fit them perfectly, so they can run their best race. It is not about giving everyone the same thing, but about giving each person what they need to succeed.

In a school setting, equity might mean providing extra support to students who need it, such as tutoring or extra time on tests, so that everyone has an equal opportunity to gain experience and succeed. It is about recognising that not everyone starts from the same place and making sure that everyone has a fair chance to reach their goals.

Overall, equity is about fairness and ensuring that everyone can thrive, regardless of their background or circumstances.

Historical context of equity

Historically, inequality has been deeply rooted in societies around the world, often stemming from factors such as race, gender, class, and other forms of identity. Here are some key points in history that illustrate the historical context of inequality:

Colonialism and slavery: Colonial powers exploited and oppressed Indigenous populations and forcibly brought Africans to the Americas as slaves. This created a legacy of racial inequality and economic disparity that persists to this day.

Civil Rights Movement: In the United States, the Civil Rights Movement of the 1950s and 1960s fought against racial segregation and discrimination, leading to significant legal and social changes. However, racial inequality and discrimination continue to be one of the key issues.

Women's rights movement: The Women's Rights Movement has fought for gender equality, including the right to vote, access to education and employment, and reproductive rights. Despite progress, gender inequality remains a global issue.

Labour rights and economic inequality: The labour movement has advocated for workers' rights and fair wages. Economic inequality, however, continues to be a major issue, with wealth and opportunity concentrated among a small percentage of the population.

Apartheid: In South Africa, apartheid was a system of institutionalised racial segregation and discrimination that was in place from 1948 to the early 1990s. The end of apartheid marked a significant victory in the fight against racial inequality.

Indigenous rights: Indigenous peoples around the world have faced historical and ongoing discrimination, displacement, and marginalisation. Efforts to recognise and protect Indigenous rights continue to be important.

Globalisation and neocolonialism: Globalisation has led to increased economic interdependence but has also resulted in growing economic inequality within and between countries. Neocolonialism, or the economic and cultural influence of powerful nations over less developed nations, has also contributed to inequality.

Understanding the historical context of inequality is crucial for addressing current issues and working towards a more just and equitable society. It highlights the need for ongoing efforts to challenge discriminatory practices, promote diversity and inclusion, and create systems that ensure fairness and opportunity for all.

Why is equity important for Youth?

Here are some examples to illustrate why equity is important for young people:

Equal access to education: Equity in education means that all young people have access to high-quality education, regardless of their background. This could include providing resources such as textbooks, computers, and internet access to students from low-income families, ensuring that they have the same opportunities to gain experience and succeed as their peers.

Equitable access to quality education, extracurricular activities, and support services enables youth to excel academically and develop important life skills.

Support for diverse needs: Equity also means providing support for young people with diverse needs. Schools and communities can offer additional tutoring or counselling services for students with learning disabilities or mental health issues, ensuring that they have the support they need to thrive academically and emotionally.

Equitable practices ensure that resources are distributed in a way that meets the diverse needs of all youth, providing them with the support they need to thrive.

Promoting diversity and inclusion: Equity in Youth organisations mean creating inclusive environments where all young people feel valued and respected.

This could include promoting diversity in leadership positions, celebrating diverse cultural traditions, and providing opportunities for young people to learn about and appreciate diverse backgrounds and perspectives.

By promoting equitable practices, we create environments that value diversity and inclusion, where every young person feels respected and valued.

Addressing systemic injustices: Equity also involves addressing systemic injustices that have disadvantaged certain groups of young people. For example, programs that aim to reduce racial disparities in school discipline or employment opportunities can help create a more equitable society for all young people.

Equity helps to dismantle systemic inequities that perpetuate discrimination and exclusion, paving the way for a more just and inclusive society.

Empowering Youth voice: Equity means empowering young people to have a voice in decisions that affect them. This could include involving young people in the planning and implementation of programs and policies that impact their lives, ensuring that their perspectives are heard and valued.

Equity ensures that the voices of all youth, including those from marginalised communities, are heard and considered in decision-making processes, empowering them to contribute to their communities.

Creating opportunities for all: Ultimately, equity is about creating opportunities for all young people to reach their full potential. By ensuring that all young people have access to the resources, support, and opportunities they need, we can create a more just, inclusive, and equitable society for everyone.

Equity ensures that all youth have access to opportunities in various areas such as education, employment, and extracurricular activities, enabling them to explore their interests and talents fully.

Analysing systemic barriers and inequalities

Despite the potential and vibrancy of Youth, they often face various systemic barriers and inequalities that hinder their development and well-being. Here is an exploration of key areas:

1. Education

Unequal access to quality education: Factors like poverty, geographical location, and systemic biases can limit access to quality education for certain groups of Youth.

This can lead to inequalities in knowledge, skills, and future opportunities.

Standardised testing: Overreliance on standardised tests can disadvantage students from diverse learning styles or backgrounds, perpetuating inequalities and limiting access to higher education or specialised programs.

Limited access to resources: Schools in underprivileged communities might lack necessary resources like technology, qualified teachers, or extracurricular activities, hindering the learning experience and impacting overall development.

2. Healthcare

Limited access to healthcare: Lack of health insurance or inadequate healthcare facilities can lead to disparities in access to preventive care, treatment, and mental health resources for certain Youth demographics.

Food insecurity: Nutritional deficiencies due to food insecurity can negatively impact physical and cognitive development, particularly among vulnerable Youth populations.

Discrimination: Biases within healthcare systems can lead to unequal treatment and disproportionate health outcomes for certain groups of Youth based on factors like race, gender, or sexual orientation.

3. Economic opportunities

Labour exploitation and trafficking: Youth, particularly from disadvantaged backgrounds, are more vulnerable to exploitation in the labour market, leading to unsafe working conditions and limited opportunities for upward mobility.

Limited job training and resources: Lack of access to job training and resources like career counselling can hinder Youth's ability to find decent work and escape poverty, perpetuating the cycle of inequality across generations.

Discrimination in hiring: Biases based on race, gender, or other factors can limit employment opportunities for certain groups of Youth, hindering their financial stability and prospects.

4. Social and environmental justice

Discriminatory policies and practices: Systemic biases within law enforcement, housing, and other societal institutions can disproportionately affect Youth from marginalised communities, limiting their access to resources and opportunities and perpetuating cycles of injustice.

Climate change and environmental degradation: The effects of climate change, such as pollution, extreme weather events, and resource scarcity, disproportionately impact younger generations, jeopardising their future and access to a healthy environment.

War and conflict: Youth living in war zones or conflict-ridden areas face heightened risks of displacement, violence, trauma, and limited access to education, healthcare, and necessities.

These are just some examples, and the specific challenges will vary depending on factors like geography, socioeconomic background, ethnicity, and gender. However, it is crucial to recognize the existence of these systemic barriers and inequalities and work towards creating a more equitable and just society where all Youth can thrive.

Equal access and opportunities for Youth

Equal access and opportunities for Youth are essential for ensuring that all can reach their full potential, regardless of their background or circumstances. Here's why equal access and opportunities are important:

Education: Education is the cornerstone of a brighter future. Equal access to quality education ensures that all youth, regardless of their socioeconomic status or geographical location, can develop their talents and pursue their dreams.

By providing equitable educational opportunities, we enable young people to break free from the cycles of poverty and marginalisation, fostering a generation of informed, skilled, and confident individuals ready to contribute to society.

Employment: Employment opportunities are vital for youth as they transition into adulthood. Equal access to meaningful, well-paying jobs ensures that all young people can build a stable future, gain independence, and contribute to the economy.

By promoting fair employment practices, providing job training, and removing barriers to employment, we empower youth to achieve their career aspirations and financial stability.

Healthcare: Health is a fundamental human right. Ensuring that all youth have access to comprehensive healthcare services, including mental health support, allows them to lead healthy, productive lives.

Equitable healthcare access means that no young person is left behind due to financial constraints, geographical barriers, or discrimination. It ensures that every youth can thrive physically, emotionally, and mentally.

Housing: Safe and stable housing is crucial for the well-being of youth. Equal access to affordable, secure housing ensures that all young people have a safe place to call home, where they can study, grow, and develop.

By addressing housing inequalities, we provide the stability that youth need to succeed in other areas of their lives, such as education and employment.

Political participation: Youth are the future leaders of our world. Equal access to political participation empowers young people to have a voice in the decisions that affect their lives and communities.

By fostering an inclusive political environment, we ensure that youth from all backgrounds can engage in civic activities, advocate for their rights, and drive social change. This promotes a more democratic and just society where every voice is heard and valued.

Social inclusion: Social inclusion is about creating environments where all youth feel welcomed, respected, and valued.

Ensuring equal access to social inclusion means breaking down barriers of discrimination and prejudice, promoting diversity, and fostering a sense of belonging. When youth are included socially, they are more likely to participate actively in their communities, build strong relationships, and develop a positive sense of self.

Closing reflections

As we conclude this chapter on the importance of equal access to essential services and opportunities for youth, let us pause to consider the transformative power of ensuring that every young person, regardless of their background, has an equal chance to succeed.

Imagine a world where all youth have access to quality education, healthcare, housing, political participation, and social inclusion. This is the world we can build together.

As we move forward, let us carry the belief that ensuring equal access to education, healthcare, housing, political participation, and social inclusion for youth is not just a moral imperative—it is a catalyst for positive change.

Be champions for equity in your schools, communities, and beyond. Advocate for policies and practices that remove barriers and create opportunities for all young people.

In ensuring equal access, we do not just change the world—we transform it. We create a future where every young person can achieve their full potential, where diversity is celebrated, and where justice prevails. This is the legacy we leave for the next generation—a legacy of equity, opportunity, and boundless potential.

Call to Action

Let us commit to being agents of equity and inclusion. Every effort we make to ensure equal access, no matter how small, contributes to a more just and equitable world. Let us start today, and let us do it together.

Thought to Ponder

How can you, in your daily life, advocate for equal access to education, healthcare, housing, political participation, and social inclusion for all youth?

By ensuring equal access, we hold the key to unlocking a world where every young person is empowered, every opportunity is available, and every future is bright. Let us make this vision a reality, one step at a time.

"Equity is the compass that guides us to fairness, ensuring each path leads to opportunity."

Chapter 4
Inclusion

"United in Diversity: Embracing Every Voice, Every Story!"

What does inclusion mean?

Inclusion refers to the practice of ensuring that all individuals, regardless of their race, gender, age, ability, religion, sexual orientation, or other characteristics, are fully participating members of a community or organisation.

Inclusion involves creating an environment where everyone feels valued, respected, and supported, and has equal access to opportunities, resources, and decision-making processes.

Inclusion goes beyond simply tolerating or accommodating differences; it involves actively seeking out and embracing diversity and creating a culture where all individuals feel that they belong and can contribute their unique perspectives and talents.

This can involve making changes to policies, practices, and attitudes that may unintentionally exclude or marginalise certain individuals and creating structures and systems that support equitable participation and representation.

Inclusion can have many positive effects, including improved social cohesion, increased creativity and innovation, better decision-making, and more positive outcomes for individuals and communities.

By promoting inclusion, we can create more just and equitable societies where all individuals can thrive and reach their full potential.

Inclusion is like a dance party where people of all backgrounds and styles come together, each adding their groove to the rhythm, making it a vibrant and unforgettable celebration!

Inclusion is like a colourful mosaic, where each piece is unique and important, but when put together, they create a beautiful and harmonious picture!

Inclusion is like a recipe with diverse ingredients, where each one adds its flavour and texture, creating a dish that is richer and more satisfying than any single ingredient alone!

Inclusion for Youth mean making sure that everyone feels welcome, valued, and respected, regardless of their differences.

Here are some simple examples to explain inclusion

School clubs: School clubs can be inclusive by ensuring that all students feel welcomed and can participate fully. For example, a drama club might adapt its activities to include students with different abilities by providing scripts in braille, using assistive listening devices, or adjusting rehearsal spaces to be wheelchair accessible.

An inclusive club also actively recruits members from diverse backgrounds, ensuring a variety of voices and experiences are represented

Sports teams: An inclusive sports team welcomes athletes of all skill levels and backgrounds. For example, a soccer team might include players from various cultural backgrounds, with the coach promoting respect and understanding of different traditions and customs.

The team might also have players with and without disabilities, playing together with adapted rules or equipment to ensure everyone can participate fully.

Classroom discussions: In an inclusive classroom, students of all abilities learn together. For instance, a student with a disability participates in the same activities as their peers, with the necessary support and accommodations.

This could mean having a sign language interpreter for a deaf student or providing extra time for tests for a student with learning disabilities. This approach ensures that every student feels valued and part of the learning community.

Community events: Inclusive community events are designed to welcome and engage everyone. For instance, a town festival might include activities and information booths celebrating various cultures, languages, and traditions within the community.

The event could offer multilingual signage and interpreters, accessible venues for people with disabilities, and activities that cater to different age groups and interests.

Friendship groups: Inclusive friendship groups welcome peers from various backgrounds, abilities, and interests. For example, a group of friends might intentionally invite classmates who might feel left out due to differences in culture, language, or abilities.

By celebrating their unique perspectives and experiences, these groups foster a sense of belonging and mutual respect.

Inclusive policies and practices: Institutions like schools, workplaces, and governments can adopt inclusive policies that promote equality and fairness. For example, a school might implement anti-bullying policies that protect all students.

A company or school might have a zero-tolerance policy for discrimination and harassment, with clear procedures for addressing complaints and supporting affected employees.

Inclusion is about creating environments where everyone feels welcomed, respected, and valued. By embracing inclusive practices in various aspects of life, we build stronger, more cohesive communities where every individual can thrive.

Inclusion is about creating a sense of belonging and ensuring that everyone can participate and contribute in their unique way.

Creating inclusive spaces

Here are some examples to elaborate on the importance of creating inclusive spaces:

Workplace inclusion: In a workplace that values inclusion, employees from diverse backgrounds feel comfortable sharing their ideas and perspectives. This can lead to greater innovation and problem-solving.

For example, a company that actively seeks input from employees of all levels and backgrounds is more likely to develop products and services that meet the needs of a diverse customer base.

Inclusive education: Inclusive education ensures that all students, regardless of their abilities or backgrounds, have access to quality education.

A school that provides accommodation for students with disabilities, such as accessible classrooms and support services, creates an inclusive learning environment where all students can thrive.

Community engagement: Inclusive community spaces, such as parks or community centres, bring people together from diverse backgrounds to participate in activities and events.

A community centre that offers programs for people of all ages and abilities promotes inclusivity and strengthens community bonds.

Online inclusion: In today's digital age, creating inclusive online spaces is also important. Social media platforms can be used to amplify diverse voices and promote understanding.

Online forums and communities that welcome people from all backgrounds can foster meaningful connections and discussions.

Cultural inclusion: Inclusive spaces also play a crucial role in promoting cultural diversity and understanding.

A museum that displays artwork from diverse cultures and provides educational programs can help visitors learn about and appreciate diversity.

In all these examples, creating inclusive spaces is not just about meeting legal or moral obligations – it is about recognising the value that diversity brings and actively working to create environments where everyone feels welcome, respected, and able to contribute their unique perspectives and talents.

The need for inclusive practices

Inclusive practices are essential for creating environments where every young person feels valued, respected, and empowered to reach their full potential. Here are several key reasons why inclusive practices are crucial for youth:

Inclusive practices benefit various settings, including schools, workplaces, and communities, by fostering a sense of belonging, promoting diversity, and improving overall outcomes.

Here are some examples:

Schools: Inclusive practices in schools create a welcoming environment for students of all backgrounds and abilities. For example, implementing inclusive education strategies helps students with disabilities learn alongside their peers, promoting empathy and understanding among students.

It also benefits students from diverse cultural backgrounds by recognizing and celebrating their unique perspectives and experiences, creating a more enriching learning environment for everyone.

Workplaces: Inclusive practices in workplaces help create a diverse and supportive atmosphere where employees feel valued and respected. For instance, promoting diversity in hiring practices ensures that people from diverse backgrounds have equal opportunities for employment and advancement.

This leads to a more innovative and productive work environment, as employees bring a wide range of perspectives and ideas to the table.

Communities: Inclusive practices in communities promote social cohesion and harmony among residents. For example, organizing community events that celebrate diverse cultures and traditions helps foster a sense of unity and belonging among residents from diverse backgrounds. It also encourages people to learn from each other and build stronger, more inclusive communities.

The need for inclusive practices for youth cannot be overstated. By embracing and promoting inclusion, we create environments where every young person can thrive. Inclusive practices are not just beneficial for individuals; they strengthen our communities, enrich our societies, and pave the way for a more just and equitable world.

As we move forward, let us commit to fostering inclusion in all areas of life, ensuring that every young person feels valued, supported, and empowered to achieve their full potential.

Intersectionality

Understanding intersectionality for youth

Intersectionality is a way of understanding how various parts of our identity come together to shape who we are and how we experience the world. It looks at how various aspects like race, gender, ability, and socio-economic status interact and influence each other. This idea helps us see that our experiences are shaped by many overlapping factors, not just one.

Easily understood examples

A young girl of colour: Imagine a young girl named Maria who is both Latina and a girl. She might face challenges that are different from those faced by a Latina boy or a White girl. For example, she might face stereotypes about her gender, like being expected to be quiet and submissive because she is a girl.

At the same time, she could encounter assumptions about her ethnicity, such as people thinking she should excel in certain subjects or activities based on her background. These combined experiences shape her unique perspective and the challenges she faces.

A boy with a disability: Think about a boy named James who uses a wheelchair and comes from a low-income family. James might face barriers related to his disability, like schools not being fully accessible, and challenges related to his family's economic situation, such as not being able to afford certain educational resources or extracurricular activities.

The combination of these factors creates a unique set of difficulties for him that would not be the same for someone who only faces one of these challenges.

A young Muslim immigrant: Imagine a young boy named Ahmed who is Muslim and an immigrant. Ahmed might face challenges related to his religion, such as needing a place to pray during the school day, and his status as an immigrant, such as language barriers or adjusting to a new culture. He might also encounter islamophobia and xenophobia, which can lead to bullying or exclusion by peers.

These intersecting identities mean Ahmed's experiences and challenges are unique, requiring specific understanding and support.

How Intersectionality Impacts Youth

Multiple layers of identity: Intersectionality helps us understand that we are not defined by just one part of our identity. For example, a young person might be a Muslim, a girl, and an immigrant. Each part of her identity affects her life in diverse ways and can create a mix of experiences that are unique to her.

She might face challenges related to her religion, gender, and immigrant status all at the same time, and these experiences can interact in complex ways.

Different experiences of discrimination: Youth can experience discrimination differently based on their intersecting identities. For instance, a Black transgender teen might face both racism and transphobia, making their experience distinct from that of a Black cisgender teen or a white transgender teen.

This means that solutions to discrimination must consider all aspects of a person's identity to be effective.

Personal strength and resilience: Recognising intersectionality also highlights the strengths and resilience that come from managing multiple identities. Youth often develop unique perspectives and critical thinking skills because they navigate various challenges simultaneously.

A young person who faces both gender discrimination and economic hardship may develop strong coping mechanisms and a deep understanding of social justice issues.

Creating inclusive environments: Understanding intersectionality helps in creating more inclusive environments. A school that recognizes intersectionality might offer support groups that address the specific needs of disabled students of color, ensuring that all aspects of their identities are acknowledged and supported. This makes the school a safer and more welcoming place for everyone.

Better support systems: When communities and institutions understand intersectionality, they can create better support systems. For instance, a community center might provide programs specifically designed for immigrant youth who are also dealing with economic challenges.

These programs can offer targeted assistance that addresses the unique combination of obstacles these young people face.

Empathy and understanding: Learning about intersectionality helps young people develop empathy and understanding for others. When youth understand that everyone has a unique combination of identities and experiences, they are more likely to be compassionate and supportive of their peers.

This can lead to stronger, more inclusive friendships and communities.

Intersectionality is about recognising and respecting the many parts of our identity that make us who we are. By understanding how these parts interact, we can better support each other and create a world where everyone feels valued and understood.

When we embrace intersectionality, we can work towards more inclusive and equitable environments for all youth, where their unique experiences and challenges are acknowledged and addressed. This not only benefits individuals but also strengthens our communities.

Closing reflections

Inclusion is not just a buzzword; it is a powerful force that transforms lives, communities, and the world. For youth, the importance of inclusion cannot be overstated. It means more than just being allowed to join in; it means feeling truly accepted and valued for who you are. It is about creating spaces where everyone, regardless of their background, ability, or identity, can thrive and reach their full potential.

Imagine a world where everyone feels they belong, where no one is left out or marginalised. This is the world we can create through inclusion. When we embrace inclusion, we tap into the richness of diverse perspectives, experiences, and ideas. We build stronger, more resilient communities where empathy and understanding flourish.

Consider the impact on a young person who feels excluded because of their race, disability, or socioeconomic status. Without inclusion, they may feel isolated, undervalued, and unable to fully participate in school, social activities, or even their dreams. But when we practice inclusion, we open doors of opportunity. We ensure that every voice is heard, every talent is recognised, and every individual can contribute to their community.

Inclusion teaches us to see beyond our differences and to appreciate the unique qualities each person brings. It challenges us to confront our biases and prejudices, step out of our comfort zones, and advocate for those who may not have a voice. By doing so, we not only help others but also enrich our own lives with new friendships, broader horizons, and deeper understanding.

Youth are the leaders of tomorrow, and the values we instill today will shape the future. By embracing inclusion now, we are planting the seeds for a world where fairness, respect, and kindness are the norm. We are building a society where everyone has the chance to succeed, and where diversity is celebrated, not just tolerated.

Call to Action

Let us commit to making inclusion a reality in our schools, communities, and everyday lives. Stand up against exclusion and discrimination whenever you see it. Be the person who reaches out to someone who feels left out.

Create spaces where every young person feels they belong, where their potential is nurtured, and where their dreams can take flight.

Thought to Ponder

Imagine how different the world would be if everyone felt truly included and valued. What can you do today to make someone feel that they belong? How can your actions contribute to a more inclusive and accepting community?

"A community thrives when every person feels seen, valued, and celebrated for their uniqueness."

Chapter 5
Creating a Sense of Belonging

"Together We Rise, By Lifting Each Other: Building A Community Of Belonging."

What does belonging mean?

Belonging means being accepted, valued, and included, regardless of one's background, identity, or circumstances. It involves creating environments where all feel they are part of the community and where their unique identities and perspectives are celebrated and respected.

Belonging

It is like feeling warm and fuzzy inside: You feel accepted, and valued, as though you are part of something bigger than yourself.

Imagine a puzzle: Each piece is unique, but they all fit together to create a beautiful picture. Belonging is when you find your place in the pussle.

It is like having a treehouse: It is your special place where you feel safe and comfortable, just like everyone deserves to feel in their community.

Here are some additional areas of belonging that can be included in the context of diversity, equity, inclusion, and belonging (DEIB):

Cultural belonging involves feeling connected to one's cultural heritage and traditions. It includes recognizing and celebrating the diverse cultural backgrounds of individuals and communities.

Social belonging relates to feeling accepted and included in social groups and networks. It involves creating environments where all Youth feel like they can make meaningful connections with others.

Academic belonging: involves feeling valued and supported in educational settings. It includes creating inclusive classrooms and schools where all students feel they can succeed academically.

Family belonging: This relates to feeling connected and supported within one's family. It includes creating family environments where all Youth feel loved, accepted, and supported.

Community belonging: This involves feeling like a valued member of one's community. It includes creating communities where all Youth feel they have a voice and can contribute to positive change.

Online belonging: This relates to feeling connected and included in online spaces. It includes creating online communities where all Youth feel safe, respected, and valued.

Environmental belonging: This involves feeling connected to and responsible for the natural environment. It includes creating environments where all Youth feel they have a role to play in protecting and preserving the planet.

Career belonging: This relates to feeling valued and included in the workplace. It includes creating work environments where all Youth feel they can pursue their career goals and contribute to their fullest potential.

By addressing these various areas of belonging, we can create more inclusive and equitable environments where all Youth feel like they belong and can thrive.

Elements of belonging

Belonging is a deep sense of connection and acceptance within a group, community, or society. It involves feeling valued, respected, and included for who you are. Several elements contribute to a sense of belonging:

Acceptance and inclusion. Feeling included and accepted within a group, community, or society, regardless of differences in background, identity, or beliefs. Being invited to join a group project at school, even if you are new to the school.

Connection to others. Building meaningful connections with others based on shared experiences, interests, or values. Making friends with someone who shares your love for a particular hobby or interest, like drawing or playing soccer.

Safety. Feeling safe and secure within your environment, both physically and emotionally. Knowing that you can speak up in class without fear of ridicule or judgment from your peers.

Identity. Being able to express your identity authentically and feeling that your identity is recognized and respected by others. Being able to wear clothing or accessories that reflect your cultural or personal identity without feeling out of place.

Support. Having access to support from others when needed and feeling that you can rely on others in times of need. You have friends who listen to you when you are feeling down and offer you encouragement and advice.

Contribution. Feeling that your contributions are valued and that you have a meaningful role within the group or community. Being recognized for your efforts in a group project and seeing how your contributions have been effective.

Shared purpose. Sharing a common purpose or goal with others creates a sense of unity and belonging. Collaborating with classmates to organise a charity event for a cause that everyone cares about.

Cultural connection. Feeling connected to your cultural heritage and traditions and being able to express and celebrate this within your community. Celebrating cultural holidays and traditions with your family and community.

Empathy and understanding. Experiencing empathy and understanding from others and extending the same empathy and understanding to others in return. Having a teacher who takes the time to listen to your concerns and helps you find solutions to problems you are facing.

When these elements are present, individuals are more likely to feel a powerful sense of belonging, which contributes to their overall well-being and sense of fulfilment. Promoting these elements of belonging can help young people feel accepted, valued, and included in their communities, and support their emotional well-being, self-esteem, and overall development.

Challenges and obstacles of not belonging

There are several challenges and obstacles that Youth may face in feeling a sense of belonging in their communities. Some of these include:

Discrimination and prejudice: Youth may face discrimination or prejudice based on their race, ethnicity, gender, sexual orientation, or other aspects of their identity. This can make us feel excluded or marginalised in our communities.

Social exclusion: Youth may feel socially excluded or isolated if they do not fit in with their peers or if they are not able to participate in social activities. This can lead to feelings of loneliness and low self-esteem.

Bullying and harassment: Bullying and harassment can create a hostile environment for Youth, making them feel unsafe and unwelcome in their communities. For example, a young person who is perceived as different from their peers may face exclusion or bullying.

Lack of representation: Youth may feel that they do not have a voice or that their experiences are not represented in their communities. This can make them feel invisible or unimportant.

Cultural barriers: Youth from limited cultural backgrounds may face cultural barriers that prevent them from fully participating in their communities. This can include language barriers, lack of access to cultural resources, or difficulty navigating cultural norms.

Socioeconomic inequality: Youth from low-income backgrounds may face barriers to belonging due to a lack of access to resources, opportunities, and social networks. This can create feelings of alienation and disconnection.

Mental health challenges: Youth who are struggling with mental health issues, such as depression or anxiety, may find it difficult to feel a sense of belonging in their communities. This can exacerbate feelings of isolation and loneliness.

Lack of supportive relationships: Youth who do not have supportive relationships with family members, peers, or other adults may struggle to feel connected to their communities. This can impact their sense of belonging and well-being.

Peer pressure: Belonging to a group can sometimes lead to peer pressure to conform to group norms. For example, a young person who relies heavily on their friendship group for validation may struggle to develop their sense of identity and autonomy.

Overall, while belonging can bring many benefits to Youth, it is important to be mindful of the challenges and to foster inclusive communities where all Youth feel accepted, valued, and supported. Addressing these challenges and obstacles requires a concerted effort from communities, schools, families, and individuals to create inclusive environments where all Youth feel valued, respected, and supported.

Benefits of belonging

Here are some Youth-related examples of the benefits of belonging:

Social support: Belonging to a group of friends or a community organisation can provide social support for Youth, helping them navigate challenges and build resilience. For example, a teenager who is part of a supportive friend group may feel more confident in dealing with peer pressure.

Identity development: Belonging to a community can help Youth develop their sense of identity. For example, a young person who participates in cultural or religious activities with their community may develop a stronger sense of cultural identity.

Mental health benefits: Belonging to a supportive community can have positive effects on Youth mental health. For example, research has shown that disabled Youth who feel a sense of belonging to their community have lower rates of depression and anxiety.

Growth opportunities: Belonging to a group or community can provide Youth with opportunities for personal and professional growth. For example, a young person who is part of a sports team may develop leadership skills and teamwork abilities.

Sense of belonging: Belonging can contribute to a sense of belonging, which is important for Youth well-being. For example, a teenager who feels accepted and valued by their peers is more likely to have positive self-esteem and mental health.

Closing reflections

Belonging is the foundation of our happiness and success. When we feel accepted, valued, and understood, we can be our true selves and achieve remarkable things. Belonging means being part of a community where our differences are celebrated and our voices are heard. It is about creating spaces where everyone feels safe, supported, and appreciated. Let us embrace the power of belonging and work together to build a world where everyone can shine.

Belonging is more than just fitting in—it is about being part of a community that values you for who you are. When we create environments that foster acceptance, value, and understanding, we unlock the potential within each of us. By embracing diversity and promoting inclusivity, we build stronger, more vibrant communities.

Call to Action

Take a moment to reach out to someone who may feel left out. Invite them to join your group, listen to their story, and celebrate their unique qualities. Small actions can create substantial changes, making everyone feel they belong.

Thought to Ponder

Imagine a world where everyone feels they belong. How would our communities look and feel if we all took steps to ensure no one is left out? What can you do today to make this vision a reality?

"Let's start now."

Chapter 6
The Impact of Stereotypes and Bias

"Look Beyond Stereotypes to See the True Diversity and Beauty in the World."

Defining stereotypes and bias
Stereotypes

A stereotype is like a sticky label that someone slaps on a whole group of people, assuming they all act, think, or look the same. It is like saying all dogs love "fetch" just because you met one enthusiastic retriever!

Stereotypes can be unfair and untrue, like thinking all teenagers are glued to their phones 24/7 (okay, maybe that one is a bit true sometimes!).

It is a generalisation or assumption about a particular group of people, based on their race, gender, age, religion, or other characteristics. Stereotypes can be positive or negative, but they are often oversimplified and can lead to inaccurate or unfair assumptions about individuals.

Stereotypes can be based on cultural or social beliefs and can perpetuate harmful prejudices and discrimination.

Bias

Bias is a bit like wearing glasses with coloured lenses. They can make you see things in a way that is not quite accurate. If you are wearing blue glasses, everything looks blue! Bias happens when you unfairly favour one thing, person, or group over another, like always picking your best friend for your team because you think they are the best, even if they have never kicked a ball straight. Bias can sneak up on you, so it is important to check if your glasses are giving you the full picture!

Bias can have a significant impact on decision-making, interactions, and relationships, and can perpetuate inequality and discrimination.

It is important to note that stereotypes and bias can intersect and reinforce each other, contributing to systemic discrimination and inequality. By recognising and challenging our own biases and stereotypes, we can work towards creating more inclusive and equitable communities.

Historical context of stereotypes and biases

Stereotypes and biases have a long and complex history, evolving alongside societal changes. Understanding this evolution can help us recognise that these beliefs are not fixed, but rather shaped by cultural, social, and political forces over time.

- In the early 20th century, many believed that women were too emotional and lacked the intellectual capacity for fields like science or politics. This stereotype was used to justify denying women the right to vote and limiting their educational opportunities.

However, as women proved these notions wrong through their achievements in various fields, these stereotypes gradually (though not completely) eroded. Today, while gender biases still exist, we see women leading nations, heading major corporations, and making groundbreaking scientific discoveries.

- Similarly, racial stereotypes have undergone significant changes. In the 19th and early 20th centuries, theories were used to justify racial hierarchies and discrimination. These harmful ideas were challenged by civil rights movements, scientific advancements in genetics, and changing social attitudes. While racial biases persist, there has been a shift toward recognising the value of diversity and the contributions of all racial groups.

- In the 1990s and early 2000s, older adults were often stereotyped as incapable of using recent technologies. Today, while some biases persist, many seniors are tech-savvy and active on social media. This shift reflects changing demographics and the existence of technology in daily life.

- Once heavily stigmatised, single parenthood is now more accepted in many societies. While challenges remain, the stereotype of the "broken home" has diminished as diverse family structures become more common and visible.

- Traditionally, men who stayed home to care for children were often viewed negatively. Today, while biases persist, there's growing acceptance of fathers taking on primary caregiving roles.

These examples demonstrate that stereotypes can and do change over time. By recognising this, young people can understand that they have the power to challenge and reshape societal attitudes, continuing the progress made by previous generations toward a more inclusive and equitable world.

Here are some examples of stereotypes and bias that Youth might encounter:

Gender stereotype: "Girls aren't good at math." This stereotype suggests that all girls are not good at math, which is not true. It can make girls feel like they should not pursue math or science-related subjects.

Racial stereotype: "All Asians are good at math." This stereotype assumes that all people of Asian descent are naturally good at math, which is not true for everyone. It can create unfair expectations and put pressure on individuals. This is also assuming someone's abilities or interests based on their race.

Religious bias: Thinking people of a certain religion all have the same beliefs or customs. A teacher might assume that a student from a certain religion is more likely to misbehave in class. This bias could lead to unfair treatment, or disciplinary actions based on the student's religion, rather than their actual behaviour.

Bias in hiring: An employer might have a bias against hiring older workers, assuming they will not be as skilled with technology. This bias could lead to qualified older candidates being overlooked for job opportunities.

Bias in friendship: A student might assume that a new classmate who speaks English as a second language will not be able to help with homework. This bias could prevent others from forming friendships and learning from each other.

Appearance bias: Judging someone's personality based on how they dress.

Practical scenario: Thinking a classmate who wears all black clothing must be unfriendly, without getting to know them.

These examples show how stereotypes and bias can lead to unfair judgments and treatment of individuals based on characteristics such as gender, race, religion, age, or language.

It is important to recognise these stereotypes and biases challenge us to promote fairness and equality for all. Youth must be aware of these stereotypes, biases, and challenges when they encounter such. By promoting diversity, inclusion, and equity, we can work towards creating more just and equitable communities for all young people.

Negative effects of stereotypes and biases

Self-esteem: Stereotypes can lower the self-esteem of individuals in stereotyped groups. For example, if a girl is constantly told that girls are not good at math, she might start to believe it and doubt her abilities.

Missed opportunities: Bias can lead to unfair treatment and missed chances for growth or achievement. A teacher might not recommend a student from a low-income background for an advanced program due to assumptions about their potential.

Limited self-perception: Youth may internalise stereotypes, limiting their aspirations and self-image. A girl might avoid pursuing a career in engineering because she has internalised the stereotype that "girls aren't good at math."

Interpersonal relationships: Biases can affect how people interact with each other. For example, if someone has a bias against people of a certain religion, they might avoid interacting with these people, leading to social isolation and division in society.

Discrimination: Stereotypes and biases can lead to discrimination, where individuals are treated unfairly or denied opportunities based on their perceived group membership. This can have long-lasting effects on their lives and well-being.

Health and well-being: Constant exposure to negative stereotypes can lead to anxiety, depression, and low self-esteem. An overweight teen might develop an eating disorder due to constant stereotyping about body image.

Perpetuation of systemic inequalities: Biases can reinforce larger societal inequalities. Employing managers might consistently favour candidates with "white sounding" names, perpetuating racial income disparities.

Limiting potential: Stereotypes and biases can limit the potential of individuals and society. When people are not given equal opportunities based on their abilities and talents, society misses their contributions and innovations.

Overall, stereotypes and biases can have far-reaching effects on Youth and society, impacting individuals' opportunities, well-being, and sense of belonging. It is important to challenge stereotypes and biases to create a more inclusive and equitable society for everyone.

Stereotypes are generally seen as negative because they oversimplify and can lead to unfair judgments or expectations.

Positive effects of stereotypes and biases

Efficiency: In certain situations, stereotypes can help people make quick decisions or judgments when they lack information. If someone is travelling to a new country and is unfamiliar with the local culture, they might rely on stereotypes to guide their behaviour.

Social cohesion: Stereotypes can sometimes help create a sense of belonging or group identity. For example, shared stereotypes about a sports team or fandom can create a sense of friendship among fans.

Cultural pride: Some positive stereotypes might contribute to cultural pride. Irish American youth might embrace stereotypes about their culture's friendliness or musical talents.

Increased awareness of diversity issues: Experiencing or witnessing stereotyping can increase awareness and motivation to address broader social issues. A student who faces gender stereotypes might become enthusiastic about promoting gender equality.

Self-expression: Some individuals may use stereotypes as a form of self-expression or cultural identity. Using stereotypical clothing or language associated with a particular group can be a way for individuals to express their identity and connect with others who share similar experiences.

It is important to note that these positive effects of stereotypes and biases are not without drawbacks. Positive stereotypes can still lead to limitations and expectations that may not be accurate or fair.

Positive biases can also lead to discrimination and inequality, disadvantaging individuals who do not fit into the preferred category.

Youth need to approach stereotypes and biases with a critical and sound perspective, recognising both the positive and negative effects, and work towards promoting diversity, inclusion, and equity in all aspects of society.

Here is what you can do:

1. Examine your own biases. Take time to reflect on your automatic assumptions and where they come from.

2. Speak up when you witness stereotyping or discrimination. Your voice matters.

3. Seek out diverse perspectives and experiences. Challenge yourself to step outside your comfort zone.

4. Educate others. Share what you have learned about stereotypes and bias with friends, family, and colleagues.

5. Support initiatives and policies that promote equality and inclusion in your school, workplace, or community.

Closing reflections

As we draw this chapter to a close, it is crucial to recognise the profound impact that stereotypes and biases can have on individuals and communities. These preconceived notions and unfair judgments can limit opportunities, stifle potential, and perpetuate division. However, by becoming aware of these biases and actively challenging them, you have the power to foster a more inclusive and equitable society.

Understanding that everyone has unique stories, experiences, and perspectives is the first step toward breaking down harmful stereotypes. Embrace diversity in all its forms and make a conscious effort to learn from and appreciate the differences among people. By doing so, you contribute to a world where everyone is valued for who they are, rather than judged by narrow and often inaccurate labels.

Call to Action

Commit to being a force for positive change by challenging stereotypes and biases in your daily life. Start by reflecting on your assumptions and making a conscious effort to see beyond them. Engage in conversations with people from diverse backgrounds, listen to their stories, and seek to understand their perspectives.

Stand up against unfair treatment and discrimination whenever you witness it and encourage others to do the same.

Your actions can inspire others to question their biases and join you in creating a more inclusive community. Remember, change begins with awareness and is propelled by action—be the catalyst for that change.

Thought to Ponder

Consider the impact of your words and actions on others. How can you use your influence to break down stereotypes and build bridges of understanding? Reflect on a time when you were judged unfairly based on a stereotype and how it made you feel. How can you ensure that others do not experience the same?

Let these reflections guide you as you strive to treat everyone with fairness, empathy, and respect. Your commitment to challenging biases not only enriches your own life but also paves the way for a more just and inclusive world.

Remember, dismantling stereotypes and overcoming bias is not a destination, but a journey. It requires constant vigilance, humility, and a willingness to grow. But with each stereotype we challenge, and each bias we overcome, we move closer to a world of true equality and understanding.

"The power to change perceptions starts with you. What will you do with that power"?

Chapter 7
You are Unique

"Embracing Your Extraordinary Self"

Youth is a vibrant explosion of potential! You are like a kaleidoscope, brimming with unique talents, perspectives, and experiences. The world craves the fresh energy and innovative ideas you bring.

Be the generation that breaks down barriers and builds bridges. Your unique spark, combined with the power of inclusivity, can illuminate the path towards a brighter future for all. So go forth, young pioneers, and paint the world with the colours of your individuality!

Ever wonder why snowflakes are all different, even though they come from the same cloud? It is because each snowflake grows uniquely, influenced by varied factors like temperature and air currents. Just like snowflakes, You are Unique!

This chapter is about celebrating that uniqueness and helping you understand how your individual qualities can shape your life and the world around you.

Your fingerprint of talents

Just as your actual fingerprint is unique to you, you possess a distinctive combination of personality, talents, interests, and experiences that set you apart from everyone else. This "talent fingerprint" is your superpower. Let us explore this idea:

Personality

Your personality is the combination of characteristics or qualities that form your distinctive character. Are you outgoing and love meeting new people, or do you prefer quiet moments with a delightful book?

Maybe you are a natural leader, or perhaps you are a great listener. Your personality traits make you who you are and play a significant role in how you interact with the world around you.

Talents

Everyone has talents, whether it is in sports, music, art, science, or something else. Think about what you excel at. Are you a talented singer, a skilled basketball player, or a math whizz kid? Talents are gifts that make you unique. They are not just about what you can do but also about what brings you joy and fulfillment.

Interests

What do you love to learn about? What hobbies do you have? Your interests shape your worldview and how you spend your time. Maybe you are fascinated by outer space, love cooking, or enjoy helping others. These interests make your life richer and more meaningful.

Experiences

Every experience, whether good or bad, teaches you something and shapes your character. Think about the time you learned to ride a bike, moved to a new school, or stood up for a friend. These moments, big and small, are part of your story. They have helped shape the unique person you are today.

How to embrace your individuality

Now that you know what makes you unique, let us discuss how to embrace it. Embracing your individuality means celebrating your identity and not trying to be someone else. Here is how you can do it:

Self-reflection: Take time to think about what makes you, YOU. Write down your strengths, interests, and what you are enthusiastic about. Reflecting on these things will help you appreciate your uniqueness. It is like looking into a mirror and seeing all the amazing things that make you special.

Be confident: Confidence is key. Believe in yourself and your abilities. Remember, no one else can be you, and that is your superpower. Stand tall, speak up, and let your voice be heard. When you are confident, you radiate a positive energy that can inspire others.

Stay true to your values: Your values are your moral compass. They guide your decisions and actions. Stay true to them, even when it is challenging. If you value honesty, be honest. If kindness is important to you, show kindness to others. Living by your values helps you stay grounded and authentic.

Embrace differences: Understand that everyone is unique, just like you. Celebrate differences and learn from others. Diversity makes the world a richer place. By appreciating the uniqueness of others, you can build stronger, more inclusive communities where everyone feels valued and respected.

Express yourself: Whether it is through fashion, art, writing, or any other form of expression, let your personality shine. Do not be afraid to stand out and be different. Wear that bright yellow jacket if it makes you happy, draw that wild painting, or author that story that has been on your mind. Expressing yourself is a powerful way to embrace your individuality.

Why being unique matters

You might wonder, "Why is it so important to be unique?" Here are a few reasons why your individuality matters:

Inspiration: When you embrace your uniqueness, you inspire others to do the same. Your confidence can light the way for someone else to be their true self. Think about the people you admire. They are probably unique in their way and have inspired you through their authenticity.

Innovation: Unique perspectives lead to innovative ideas. The world needs diverse thinkers to solve problems and create new opportunities. Your unique way of thinking can contribute to advancements in technology, art, science, and so much more. Innovation often comes from those who dare to think differently.

Authentic connections: When you are true to yourself, you attract people who appreciate you for who you are. This leads to deeper, more meaningful relationships. Authentic connections are built on trust and mutual respect. By being yourself, you create an environment where others feel comfortable being themselves too.

Personal growth: Embracing your individuality helps you grow as a person. You learn more about yourself and become more resilient and self-assured. Each step you take in your journey of self-discovery adds to your personal growth. You become more aware of your strengths and areas for improvement, leading to continuous development.

Happiness: Being true to yourself leads to greater happiness and fulfillment. You are not living a life to please others but one that brings you joy and satisfaction. When you embrace who you are, you align your life with your true desires and passions, leading to a more fulfilling and happy existence.

Wake up and shine

It is time to wake up from the slumber of conformity and shine as the unique individual you are. Remember, you are a one-of-a-kind masterpiece, and the world is waiting to see your brilliance. Embrace your quirks, celebrate your talents, and be proud of your journey. You have the power to have influence simply by being YOU.

Here are some practical steps to help you wake up and shine:

1. Set goals: Set goals that align with your passions and values. Whether it is learning a new skill, starting a project, or making new friends, having goals gives you a sense of purpose and direction.

Setting goals is a powerful way to focus your energy and achieve your dreams. When you set goals, you create a roadmap for your future and give yourself something to strive for. Here is how to set effective goals and stay motivated:

2. Identify your passions: Start by identifying what you are enthusiastic about. What activities make you lose track of time? What topics do you love to learn about? Your passions can guide you toward setting meaningful goals that align with your interests and values.

3. Set SMART goals: Make your goals Specific, Measurable, Achievable, Relevant, and Time-bound (SMART). For example, instead of saying, "I want to be better at math," set a SMART goal like, "I will improve my math skills by practicing for 30 minutes every day and aim to score an A on my next exam."

4. Break it down: Big goals can sometimes feel overwhelming. Break them down into smaller, manageable steps. If your goal is to author a book, start with writing one page a day. Smaller milestones make the journey more manageable and keep you motivated.

5. Create a plan: Develop a detailed plan outlining the steps you need to take to achieve your goal. Include deadlines for each step to keep yourself on track. A clear plan can help you stay organised and focused.

6. Stay flexible: Life is unpredictable, and sometimes you may need to adjust your goals or the steps to achieve them. Be flexible and open to change. Adaptability is a key part of achieving long-term success.

Take care of yourself

Self-care is essential to embracing your uniqueness. When you prioritise your well-being, you are better equipped to manage life's challenges and fully express your individuality. Here are some self-care tips to help you shine your brightest:

1. Physical health: Exercise regularly, eat nutritious foods, and get enough sleep. Taking care of your body gives you the energy and strength to pursue your passions and dreams.

2. Mental health: Take time to relax and de-stress. Practice mindfulness or meditation to stay grounded and focused. If you ever feel overwhelmed, do not hesitate to talk to someone you trust, like a friend, family member, or counselor.

3. Emotional health: Acknowledge your feelings and do not bottle them up. It is okay to feel sad, angry, or frustrated sometimes. Expressing your emotions in healthy ways, like talking, writing, or creating art, helps you process and move forward.

4. Self-compassion: Be kind to yourself. Everyone makes mistakes and has flaws. Instead of being overly critical, practice self-compassion. Treat yourself with the same kindness and understanding you would offer a friend.

Keep learning

Never stop learning and exploring. Continuous learning helps you grow and discover new facets of your uniqueness. Here are some ways to keep your curiosity alive:

1. Read widely: Books, articles, and blogs can open your mind to innovative ideas and perspectives. Choose topics that interest you and challenge yourself to think differently.

2. Start hobbies: Trying new hobbies can reveal hidden talents and passions. Whether it is playing a musical instrument, painting, coding, or gardening, hobbies add depth to your personality.

3. Explore the world: If you have the opportunity, travel to unfamiliar places. Experiencing diverse cultures and environments can broaden your understanding of the world and your place in it.

4. Ask questions: Do not be afraid to ask questions and seek answers. Curiosity leads to discovery, and discovery leads to growth.

Surround yourself with positivity

The people you surround yourself with have a significant impact on your life. Choose to be around those who uplift and support you. Here is how to create a positive environment:

1. Positive relationships: Build relationships with people who encourage and inspire you. Friends and mentors who believe in you can boost your confidence and help you stay true to yourself.

2. Avoid negativity: Distance yourself from negative influences. People who constantly criticize or bring you down can hinder your growth. Seek constructive feedback, but do not let negativity dampen your spirit.

3. Create a support system: Have a group of people you can turn to for advice, encouragement, and support. This network can provide strength and perspective when you need it most.

4. Spread positivity: Be a positive influence in others' lives. Your kindness and support can create a ripple effect, making your community a better place.

Give back

Using your unique talents and experiences to help others not only benefits those in need but also enriches your own life. Here are some ways to give back:

1. Volunteer: Find a cause you are enthusiastic about and dedicate some time to it. Volunteering can be a rewarding way to have influence and meet like-minded people.

2. Mentor: Share your knowledge and experiences with others. Whether it is helping a younger student, guiding a peer, or offering advice to someone starting in your field, mentoring can be a powerful way to give back.

3. Acts of Kindness: Small acts of kindness can have a significant impact. Whether it is helping a neighbour, donating to a charity, or simply offering a smile, your actions can brighten someone's day.

4. Community Involvement: Get involved in your community. Attend local events, join clubs or organisations, and participate in initiatives that improve your surroundings.

Youth heroes who used their talents to have influence

Youth have incredible potential to create positive change in the world. Here are some inspiring examples of young individuals who have used their unique talents and passions to make a significant impact.

1. Nkosi Johnson: Born with HIV in South Africa, Nkosi became a powerful voice for HIV/AIDS awareness and education. By age 11, he had addressed the International AIDS Conference and challenged the South African government to provide antiretroviral drugs to pregnant women with HIV. His unique perspective as a child living with HIV allowed him to touch hearts and change minds in ways adults could not.

2. Boyan Slat: At 16, Boyan combined his passion for engineering and his concern for the environment to tackle ocean plastic pollution. He invented a system that uses ocean currents to collect plastic, founding The Ocean Cleanup at 18. His unique approach has now removed millions of kilograms of plastic from the ocean.

3. Gitanjali Rao: Named Time Magazine's first-ever "Kid of the Year" at

15, Gitanjali has invented solutions for detecting lead in drinking water, preventing cyberbullying, and diagnosing opioid addiction. Her unique talent lies in applying technology to solve real-world problems.

4. Marley Dias: At 11, Marley loved reading but was frustrated by the lack of books featuring Black girls as main characters. Her passion for diverse representation led her to start the #1000BlackGirlBooks campaign, which has collected over 12,000 books featuring Black female protagonists.

5. Ann Makosinski: At 15, Ann invented a flashlight powered by the heat of the human hand, inspired by a friend in the Philippines who could not study at night due to lack of electricity. Her unique combination of engineering skills and desire to help others led to this innovative solution.

These heroes, as youth, remind us that age is no barrier to making a difference. Their unique talents, dedication, and courage have brought about meaningful change in various fields. What talents do you have, and how can you use them to make a positive impact? The world needs your unique contributions!

These young people have transformed their passions into powerful forces for change. They have faced adversity, stood up against injustice, and used their talents to create a better world. Their stories are not just tales of exceptional individuals but powerful reminders that within each of us lies the ability to be a force for good.

Embrace your talents, avoid destructive paths

Each one of you is unique, possessing a blend of talents, interests, and dreams that no one else in the world has. This uniqueness is your superpower, something that can lead you to accomplish amazing things. However, it is important to remember that the choices you make every day can either help your talents flourish or stifle them completely.

Nurture your talents

Imagine your talents and interests as seeds. To grow into strong, beautiful trees, they need care, attention, and the right environment. This means investing your time and energy into positive activities that help you learn and grow.

Join clubs, participate in sports, start hobbies, or volunteer for causes you care about. These positive experiences will help you develop your skills, build confidence, and form healthy relationships.

The importance of Diversity, Equity, Inclusion, and Belonging to enhance Youth talent, interests and experiences

Diversity, equity, inclusion, and belonging (DEIB) are crucial elements in nurturing and developing youth talent, interests, and experiences. Here is why:

1. Diversity enriches learning: Exposure to diverse cultures, perspectives, and ideas helps youth develop a broader understanding of the world. This exposure can spark new interests and inspire creativity by showing young people the many ways to approach problems and think about solutions.

2. Equity ensures fair opportunities: When everyone has access to the same resources and opportunities, regardless of their background, all youth have the chance to pursue their talents and interests. Equity helps to level the playing field, ensuring that no one is held back by systemic barriers or personal circumstances.

3. Inclusion fosters collaboration: When young people feel included, they are more likely to participate actively and collaborate with others. Inclusive environments encourage teamwork and the sharing of ideas, which can lead to innovative projects and a deeper understanding of various subjects.

4. Belonging boosts confidence and motivation: Feeling a sense of belonging is essential for young people's emotional well-being. When youth feel accepted and valued for who they are, they are more likely to take risks, try new things, and fully engage in activities. This sense of belonging can significantly enhance their talents and interests.

5. DEIB prepares Youth for the future: In a globalised world, understanding and valuing diversity is critical. Youth who are well-versed in DEIB principles are better prepared for future workplaces and communities that are increasingly diverse. This preparation can enhance their career prospects and ability to navigate complex social environments.

6. Encourages empathy and social responsibility: Learning about and valuing diversity, equity, inclusion, and belonging helps young people develop empathy and a sense of social responsibility. These qualities are essential for creating a more just and equitable society. Youth who understand and practice DEIB are more likely to become advocates for positive change in their communities.

7. Enhances critical thinking skills: Diverse teams bring a variety of perspectives to the table, which can lead to more effective problem-solving. When youth work in diverse groups, they learn to appreciate different viewpoints and develop skills in critical thinking and collaboration.

8. Supports personal growth: Engaging with DEIB concepts helps youth explore their own identities and understand their place in the world. This exploration can lead to greater self-awareness and personal growth, empowering young people to pursue their passions with confidence and purpose.

Incorporating DEIB principles into youth development programs, education, and community activities is essential for creating environments where all young people can thrive. By embracing these values, we can help youth develop their talents, pursue their interests, and gain experiences that will benefit them throughout their lives.

The Trap of destructive deeds

Sometimes, the journey can get tough, and you might feel tempted to take shortcuts or engage in negative behaviours. Destructive deeds, like skipping school, bullying others, discrimination, using drugs, or giving in to peer pressure, may seem like quick fixes or ways to fit in, but they have profound consequences.

When you engage in these behaviours, you risk your health and well-being and your future. You could miss opportunities to display your talents, gain new skills, and achieve your goals.

Bad attitudes and negativity can drive away friends, mentors, and supporters who would otherwise help you on your journey.

Real-life consequences

Consider the story of Alex, a talented young musician with a bright future. Alex was enthusiastic about playing the guitar and dreamt of starting a band. However, he got involved with a group of friends who were more interested in partying and causing trouble than in supporting his musical ambitions.

Alex started skipping music practice, his grades dropped, and he even got into legal trouble. As a result, he lost his scholarship to a prestigious music school and had to spend years rebuilding his life and reputation.

On the other hand, there is the story of Maya, who also faced challenges and temptations. Maya loved science and dreamed of becoming a doctor. Despite peer pressure to skip classes and engage in risky behaviours, she stayed focused on her studies and sought out positive influences.

Maya volunteered at a local clinic, joined a science club, and surrounded herself with friends who supported her goals. Today, Maya is well on her way to achieving her dream of making a difference in her community as a doctor.

Both Alex's and Maya's stories highlight the importance of making positive choices and staying true to your values. By embracing diversity, equity, inclusion, and belonging, you can create a supportive environment for yourself and others, fostering a sense of community and shared success.

Choosing positivity

You have the power to choose your path. Surround yourself with positive influences – people who encourage you to pursue your dreams and who celebrate your successes.

Stay committed to your goals, and do not let negativity or bad attitudes pull you down. Remember, every challenge you face is an opportunity to gain experience stronger and more resilient.

Embrace DEIB in your journey. Celebrate your unique talents and those of others. Ensure that everyone in your circle feels valued and included, and advocate for fairness and equity in all your endeavours. This approach not only benefits you but also contributes to a more inclusive and supportive community for everyone.

Closing reflections

The journey of making a difference starts with a single step, and that step begins with you. Embrace your uniqueness, set bold goals, and act. The world needs your voice, your ideas, and your passion.

Just like the young heroes we have met in this chapter, you have the power to inspire change, uplift others, and leave a lasting impact.

In a world that often feels dominated by the actions of adults, these young heroes prove that age is not a limit to making a difference. Their stories of courage, innovation, and unwavering dedication to their causes inspire us all to look within ourselves and recognise our unique potential.

Your uniqueness is a gift to the world. By making positive choices, staying true to your values, and avoiding destructive paths, you can nurture your talents and achieve incredible things. Believe in yourself, stay focused, and remember that you are capable of greatness.

The world is waiting for your unique contributions, so shine brightly and let your talents bloom.

In your journey, never forget the importance of diversity, equity, inclusion, and belonging. By fostering an environment where everyone feels valued and included, you can make a positive impact on your community and beyond. Embrace your uniqueness, support others in their journeys, and together, you can create a brighter, more inclusive future.

Call to Action

Take a moment today to think about what truly matters to you. Identify a cause that resonates with your heart. Whether it is helping those in need, protecting the environment, or standing up for justice, commit to taking one small step toward making a difference.

Volunteer, start a project, raise awareness—your actions, no matter how small, can create a ripple effect of positive change.

Thought to Ponder

What would the world look like if everyone embraced their unique talents and passions to be effective? Imagine the collective power of individuals, each contributing their unique strengths to create a world of compassion, innovation, and justice.

As you reflect on these young heroes, consider the talents and passions that make you unique. What issues do you care deeply about? How can you use your skills to make a positive impact in your community, your country, or even the world?

Remember, you do not need superpowers to be a hero—just a heart full of compassion, a mind open to possibilities, and the courage to act.

Remember, you are one of a kind, and your potential to be effective is limitless.

"So, rise, young hero. Your story is just beginning. The world is waiting for the difference only you can make."

Chapter 8
Our Connected World

The Superpowers of Diversity, Equity, Inclusion and Belonging

Globalisation

Globalisation means the growing interconnectedness of the world. Countries trade with each other, people travel all over the globe, and ideas are shared instantly, thanks to technology. It is like the world becoming one giant neighbourhood!

We are living in the most globally interconnected era in human history. Rapidly evolving technologies have enabled the free flow of information, ideas, capital, goods, services, and people across borders like never before. This phenomenon, known as globalisation, has had profound and wide-ranging impacts on the world's economies, cultures, environments, and societies. For today's young people coming of age in this globalising world, both the opportunities and challenges are immense.

Globalisation is like making the world a smaller place. It is about how people, businesses, and countries are becoming more connected. Imagine the Earth as a big puzzle. Globalisation is like fitting the pieces together more tightly, so we can see and interact with each other better.

How does it happen?

Globalisation happens in many ways:

Trade: Countries exchange goods and services. For example, your favorite jeans might be made in one country but sold in another.

Technology: The internet and smartphones connect people from all over the world. We can talk, share ideas, and do business with people on the other side of the planet.

Travel: Planes, trains, and cars make it easier for people to visit different countries. This helps us learn about other cultures and share our own.

Investment: Businesses from one country can invest in businesses in another country. This helps create jobs and grow economies.

Examples of globalisation

Fast food: You can find popular fast-food chains in many countries. This shows how businesses spread across the world.

Music: Music styles from diverse cultures are shared worldwide. You can listen to music from any country on your phone.

Sports: International sports events like the Olympics bring people together from all over the world.

The opportunities of a globalised world for Youth

Globalisation has vastly expanded the horizons and possibilities for younger generations compared to any time before. Some of the key opportunities include:

Access to global education and careers. Thanks to the internet and innovations in remote learning, young people today can receive world-class education from prestigious universities and training programs globally without leaving their home country.

International companies also offer an array of remote work opportunities across diverse cultures and time zones.

Fostering global competencies. Growing up exposed to global flows of information, diverse cultures, and internationally connected social networks prepares Youth to thrive in our multicultural, multilingual 21st-century world.

Key competencies like cross-cultural communication, digital literacy, critical thinking, and problem-solving across differences are instilled from an early age.

Sharing ideas and driving change. New communication technologies have empowered Youth to share ideas, creativity, and innovations with global audiences.

From social media to open-source projects, young voices advocating for change on issues like climate change, human rights, and equality of opportunity can be elevated worldwide.

Exploring and appreciating cultural diversity. With the increased mobility of people and a globally connected internet culture, teenagers are exposed to the world's diverse cultures, art forms, foods, perspectives, and ways of life.

This fosters open-mindedness, curiosity, deeper human connections, and an appreciation of our differences.

Entrepreneurial opportunities in the global economy. Globalised free markets create vast entrepreneurial opportunities for young creators, innovators, and business builders to bring their ideas and products to a world marketplace.

Apps, creative works, and services can find audiences and investors around the globe more easily than ever before.

The challenges of globalisation for Youth

Navigating the complex landscape of globalisation presents significant challenges for youth, as they must adapt to rapid cultural, technological, and economic changes while striving to maintain their unique identities and values. These young individuals face the pressure of staying competitive in a global job market, overcoming digital divides, and managing the impacts of climate change and socio-economic disparities.

Additionally, they must grapple with cultural integration which can erode local traditions and languages, while also finding ways to advocate for social justice and equality in an interconnected world.

Economic disruptions and job insecurity. As industries, companies, and labour markets globalise, many existing jobs get outsourced or made obsolete by automation and efficiency initiatives.

This makes achieving stable, well-paying employment more precarious, especially for those without in-demand technical skills or higher education.

Rising inequality and competition. While economic globalisation has lifted millions out of poverty, it has simultaneously widened inequalities between the global "winners" with access to opportunities versus those left behind without.

This puts immense pressure on Youth to outcompete peers globally to secure the limited pathways to success.

Cultural integration and identity struggles. With multinational corporations marketing their consumer cultures worldwide and the global spread of social media, there are concerns about traditional cultures being eroded and dominated by Western/American pop culture norms and values.

This can create challenging identity struggles for Youth trying to balance local heritage with global influences.

The environmental toll of globalisation. While globalisation has enabled more efficient production and distribution, critics argue this has come through unsustainable exploitation of the environment and natural resources.

Youth will extremely face the destructive impacts of the globalisation-fuelled climate crisis like rising sea levels, extreme weather events, mass human displacement, and food/water shortages.

Global spread of misinformation and divisive politics. The global internet has created a virtually unregulated space where misinformation, extremist ideologies, hate speech, identity-based nationalism, and polarising political movements can proliferate rapidly across borders.

This is brainwashing some Youth populations and fuelling societal conflicts.

Navigating the globalising world

Globalisation is an enormously complex, multifaceted force profoundly reshaping the reality for today's young people. To constructively navigate this globalising world, educational institutions, families, and Youth must focus on developing key skills and mindsets.

Navigating the globalising world can be challenging for youth, but there are several strategies they can employ to thrive in this dynamic environment. Here are some practical examples:

1. Embrace Lifelong Learning

   - Example: Enrol in online courses or attend workshops to acquire new skills, such as coding, digital marketing, or foreign languages. Platforms like Coursera, Khan Academy, and Duolingo offer valuable resources to enhance knowledge and stay competitive in the global job market.

2. Cultivate Cultural Competence

   - Example: Participate in exchange programs, travel abroad, or engage in local cultural events to learn about diverse cultures and perspectives. Joining clubs or organisations that celebrate diversity can also help youth develop a deeper understanding and appreciation for global cultures.

3. Leverage technology for connection and learning

   - Example: Use social media and other digital platforms to connect with peers from around the world. Engage in online forums, virtual study groups, or collaborative projects that bring together diverse perspectives and foster global friendships.

4. Develop critical thinking and critical thinking skills

   - Example: Participate in debate clubs or problem-solving competitions like hackathons. These activities encourage youth to think critically about global issues and develop innovative solutions.

5. Advocate for social and environmental causes

   - Example: Get involved in community service projects or global initiatives that address social justice, climate change, or poverty. Organisations like Amnesty International, UNICEF, and local NGOs offer opportunities for youth to make a positive impact on the world.

6. Foster entrepreneurship and innovation

   - Example: Start a small business, launch a blog, or create a YouTube channel to share unique ideas and talents with a global audience. Programs like Junior Achievement or local incubators can provide mentorship and resources for young entrepreneurs.

7. Build a dedicated support network

- Example: Join youth groups, mentorship programs, or professional organisations that offer guidance, support, and opportunities for personal and professional growth. Networks like the Global Shapers Community or local youth councils can provide valuable connections and resources.

8. Stay informed about global issues

- Example: Follow reputable news sources, read books, and attend lectures or webinars to stay updated on current global events and trends. Understanding the broader context of global challenges helps youth make informed decisions and become active global citizens.

By adopting these strategies, youth can effectively navigate the complexities of a globalising world, build resilience, and position themselves for success in an interconnected future.

How do we make this global game work for everyone?

That is where the superpowers of Diversity, Equity Inclusion, and Belonging come in!

Example: Think of a soccer team:

Diversity: Each player brings different skills and experiences – speed, strategy, amazing footwork! This diverse set of strengths makes the team stronger.

Equity: Everyone can play, regardless of their background or how much they practice. The rules are the same for everyone.

Inclusion: Creating a supportive and welcoming environment where everyone can feel they belong and can contribute to the team's success.

Belonging: The team feels like a family, with members supporting each other and celebrating each other's wins.

Just like a great soccer team, the world benefits when we:

Celebrate our differences: From K-pop music to traditional African dance, there's so much cool stuff to discover in diverse cultures! We can learn, share, and appreciate each other's unique ways of doing things.

Play fair: Everyone deserves equal opportunities, no matter where they come from or what they look like. Imagine online games where everyone has access to the same resources – that is what fair play looks like in the real world too!

Make everyone feel welcome: The coolest online game loses it is fun if half the players are not welcome to join. In a globalised world, everyone deserves a sense of belonging, feeling safe, respected, and part of something bigger than us.

The superpowers of a globalised World

Diversity, Equity, Inclusion and Belonging are not just buzzwords – they are crucial to making globalisation work for everyone. Think of us as the superpowers, we need to address challenges, create opportunities, and build a more just and peaceful world. Here is how:

Superpower #1: Innovation and creativity

When people from diverse backgrounds with diverse knowledge and viewpoints work together, we see an explosion of innovative ideas!

Just like combining different ingredients in a recipe creates interesting flavours, diverse teams produce better solutions to problems.

Superpower #2: Economic strength

Companies and countries that embrace diversity and fairness attract the best talent from around the world.

Happy and fulfilled employees or citizens create a stronger, more productive, and successful economy.

Superpower #3: Cultural exchange and understanding

Globalisation brings us closer to diverse cultures, promoting respect and understanding.

Learning from each other breaks down stereotypes, helps us become more tolerant, and makes the world more peaceful.

Superpower #4: Resilience

Diverse communities are more resilient to crises. Just like a forest with different tree types is stronger when facing storms, a diverse society with a variety of skills and perspectives can better adapt and overcome challenges.

Here are why these superpowers are epic:

Innovation explosion: Imagine a group project where everyone brings different ideas to the table. The more diverse the group, the cooler and more creative the final project can be!

Global dream team: When talented people from diverse backgrounds work together, amazing things can happen. Just like doctors from different countries collaborating to find cures for diseases!

Peace and understanding: When we understand and respect diverse cultures, we break down stereotypes and build bridges of friendship. This can help prevent conflicts and create a more peaceful world.

Closing reflections

Globalisation is more than just a buzzword; it is the heartbeat of our interconnected world. It is a complex interplay of economics, culture, technology, and politics that has reshaped societies and economies. From the clothes we wear to the food we eat; globalisation touches every aspect of our lives.

This interconnectedness brings both immense opportunities and significant challenges. It can foster economic growth, cultural exchange, and innovation. Yet, it can also worsen inequalities, environmental issues, and foreign affairs tensions.

You, the next generation, are uniquely positioned to navigate this complex landscape. Your digital fluency, your global perspective, and your passion for a better world are essential to shaping a more just, equitable, and sustainable future.

Call to Action

You, the young generation, are the architects of tomorrow's global landscape. Your understanding of globalisation is crucial. It is time to step into the spotlight. Be curious explorers of this interconnected world.

Question the status quo, challenge inequalities, and advocate for a more just and sustainable global community. Your voice matters. Use it to inspire change, to bridge divides, and to create a world where everyone thrives.

Thought to Ponder

Globalisation is not just about economics or technology. It is about humanity. It is about recognising our shared responsibility to care for our planet and it is people. It is about building bridges, not walls.

Remember, you are a global citizen.

Your actions have ripples that extend far beyond your community. Embrace the challenges, celebrate the diversity, and shape a future where globalisation is a force for good. The world is waiting for your vision.

Are you ready to be a catalyst for change?

Chapter 9

Looking Towards the Future

"Shape Your Tomorrow, Today! The Future is Yours to Create."

As the world rapidly changes, the future holds endless possibilities for youth. Technological advancements, societal shifts, and environmental changes are just a few of the factors that will shape the world you will inherit. This chapter delves into the trends that are likely to influence the future and explores how you, can prepare to thrive in this evolving landscape.

The rise of technology

Technology is evolving at a remarkable pace, transforming the way we live, work, and communicate. Consider the following trends:

Artificial intelligence (AI): AI is becoming increasingly integrated into our daily lives. From virtual assistants like Siri and Alexa to more complex applications like self-driving cars and medical diagnostics, AI is poised to revolutionise numerous industries.

Imagine a future where AI helps in personalising education, making learning more accessible and tailored to individual needs.

Virtual and augmented reality (VR/AR): These technologies are creating remarkable experiences that blend the digital and physical worlds. Think of how VR can transform classrooms, allowing students to explore historical events or distant planets as if they were there. AR, on the other hand, can enhance real-world experiences, such as providing real-time translations or interactive museum tours.

VR experiences foster empathy by allowing individuals to "walk in another person's shoes", experiencing different perspectives first-hand.

Sustainable technology: With the growing awareness of climate change, there is a surge in developing technologies aimed at sustainability. Innovations like solar power, electric vehicles, and biodegradable materials are just the beginning.

Imagine a future where cities are powered by renewable energy, reducing our carbon footprint and preserving the planet for future generations.

Social and cultural shifts

As the world becomes more interconnected, social and cultural trends are also evolving.

Here are a few to consider:

Global citizenship: With the internet breaking down geographical barriers, young people are becoming global citizens. This means embracing diverse cultures, advocating for social justice, and working towards common goals such as peace and equality.

Think of how social media platforms allow you to connect with peers from around the world, sharing ideas and collaborating on projects that can drive positive change.

Inclusivity and Diversity: The future is about celebrating differences and ensuring that everyone has a seat at the table. Movements advocating for gender equality and racial justice are gaining momentum.

Youth, you can play a pivotal role by promoting inclusivity in your communities, schools, and workplaces. Imagine a future where everyone feels valued and respected, regardless of their background or identity.

Mental health awareness: There is a growing recognition of the importance of mental health. Initiatives aimed at reducing stigma and increasing access to mental health resources are crucial.

Picture a future where mental health is treated with the same importance as physical health, with widespread support systems in place to help those in need.

Environmental stewardship

The future of our planet is in your hands.

Here are some environmental trends to be aware of:

Climate change action: The effects of climate change are becoming more apparent, and the need for action is urgent. From reducing carbon emissions to protecting endangered species, there is much work to be done.

Imagine a future where renewable energy sources replace fossil fuels, and sustainable practices are the norm in agriculture, manufacturing, and daily life.

Conservation efforts: Protecting natural habitats and preserving biodiversity is crucial for a healthy planet. Initiatives such as reforestation, marine conservation, and wildlife protection are gaining traction.

Imagine a future where humans live in harmony with nature, ensuring that ecosystems thrive for generations to come.

Sustainable living: Adopting sustainable lifestyles can have a significant impact on the environment. This includes reducing waste, recycling, and supporting eco-friendly products.

Picture a future where communities are built around principles of sustainability, with green spaces, clean air, and abundant natural resources.

Future trends to watch

1. Digital transformation and AI

The integration of artificial intelligence (AI) and machine learning into various industries is accelerating. Youth must stay informed about advancements in AI, automation, and data science, as these technologies will reshape job markets, education, and daily life.

- Example: Learning to code, understanding AI ethics, and staying updated on the latest tech innovations will be crucial for future career opportunities.

2. Sustainability and green technologies

As the world grapples with climate change, sustainable practices and green technologies will become increasingly important. Youth should be aware of trends in renewable energy, sustainable agriculture, and eco-friendly products.

- Example: Getting involved in environmental activism, studying environmental science, or pursuing careers in green technology can position youth as leaders in the fight against climate change.

3. Remote work and gig economy

The rise of remote work and the gig economy is transforming traditional employment models. Youth need to adapt to flexible working conditions and explore opportunities in freelancing, remote jobs, and entrepreneurship.

- Example: Developing skills in digital communication, project management, and self-discipline can help youth thrive in this evolving work environment.

4. Mental health awareness

Mental health is gaining more attention, and there is a growing emphasis on well-being and self-care. Youth should stay informed about mental health trends, resources, and strategies to maintain their emotional and psychological well-being.

- Example: Engaging in mindfulness practices, seeking therapy, and promoting mental health awareness in communities can contribute to a healthier society.

5. Social and political activism

Youth are increasingly engaged in social and political activism, advocating for change on issues like racial justice, gender equality, and human rights. Staying informed about social movements and political trends is essential.

- Example: Participating in protests, joining advocacy groups, or using social media platforms to raise awareness and mobilise action can amplify youth voices in shaping policy and societal norms.

6. Global health initiatives

The COVID-19 pandemic has highlighted the importance of global health initiatives and the need for resilient healthcare systems. Youth should pay attention to trends in public health, vaccination efforts, and global health policy.

   - Example: Studying public health, volunteering in health-related organisations, or supporting global health campaigns can prepare youth to contribute to future health challenges.

7. Personalised education

Education is becoming more personalised, with adaptive learning technologies and tailored educational pathways. Youth should explore opportunities for personalised learning experiences that cater to their interests and strengths.

   - Example: Utilising online learning platforms, engaging in self-directed learning, and seeking mentorship can help youth maximise their educational potential.

8. Blockchain and cryptocurrency

Blockchain technology and cryptocurrencies are disrupting traditional finance and creating new opportunities in decentralised finance (DeFi). Youth should understand the basics of blockchain, cryptocurrency, and their potential applications.

   - Example: Investing in cryptocurrencies, learning about blockchain technology, and exploring careers in fintech can position youth at the forefront of financial innovation.

By staying informed about these future trends, youth can proactively adapt to changes, seise new opportunities, and play a pivotal role in shaping the future.

Challenges and opportunities for Youth

The future poses a complex array of challenges and opportunities for youth, from grappling with the impacts of climate change and navigating an increasingly digitalised job market to leveraging technological innovations and advocating for social justice, all of which demand resilience, adaptability, and initiative-taking engagement to shape a better world.

Challenges

While the future holds great promise, there are also significant challenges that youth will face:

Digital divide: Despite technological advancements, access to technology remains unequal. Many young people, especially in underprivileged communities, lack access to reliable internet and digital devices.

While connecting the world, the unregulated tech spaces have also enabled the spread of misinformation, hate speech, and divisive foreign affairs movements that are radicalising some Youth populations

This digital divide can hinder education and job opportunities. Addressing this disparity is crucial for ensuring that all youth can benefit from technological progress.

Climate anxiety: The looming threat of climate change can cause significant anxiety and stress among young people. Feeling overwhelmed by the vastness of the problem can lead to a sense of helplessness.

It is important to channel this anxiety into positive action and to support each other in advocating for sustainable practices and policies.

Economic uncertainty: The job market is evolving rapidly, with many traditional jobs being replaced by automation and new industries emerging. This can create uncertainty about future career prospects.

AI and automation threaten to displace many traditional jobs and career paths as robots/software take over human tasks. This makes achieving stable, well-paying employment precarious without in-demand technical skills.

Preparing for this changing landscape through continuous learning and adaptability will be essential.

Mental health challenges: Despite increased awareness, mental health issues among youth are on the rise. Social media, academic pressures, and global uncertainties contribute to this trend.

Access to mental health resources and creating supportive environments are key to addressing these challenges.

Opportunities

Alongside these challenges, there are numerous opportunities for youth to seize:

Entrepreneurship and innovation: The digital age offers exceptional opportunities for entrepreneurship. With access to global markets and digital tools, young people can start businesses, create apps, and develop innovative solutions to pressing problems.

Imagine a future where you turn your passion into a successful venture that makes a positive impact on the world.

Advocacy and activism: Youth have always been at the forefront of social change. From climate strikes to movements for racial justice, young people are leading the charge. Use your voice and platforms to advocate for issues you care about and inspire others to join the cause.

Picture a future where your activism leads to tangible changes in policies and societal norms.

Global collaboration: The interconnected world allows for unprecedented collaboration across borders. Engage in international projects, cultural exchanges, and global initiatives.

Imagine a future where you collaborate with peers from different countries to solve global challenges and foster mutual understanding.

Skills development: The future job market will require a diverse set of skills, including digital literacy, critical thinking, and emotional intelligence. Embrace opportunities to gain experience and grow in these areas.

Imagine a future where your diverse skill set opens doors to exciting career paths and opportunities.

Preparing for the future

Preparing for the future is not just about adapting to change—it is about driving that change. It is about being bold in the face of uncertainty, resilient when facing obstacles, and visionary in crafting solutions that will benefit not only yourself but also society.

Youth possess the extraordinary power to shape the future, harnessing their creativity, energy, and innovative spirit to drive social, technological, and environmental advancements.

Through their unique perspectives and relentless pursuit of change, they challenge the status quo, advocate for social justice, and push for policies that address pressing global issues such as climate change, inequality, and human rights.

Youth have the power to shape the future. Here are some ways to prepare:

Education and lifelong learning: Stay curious and keep learning. The skills needed for the future are constantly evolving, so embrace opportunities for continuous education. Think about how online courses and digital resources can help you acquire new skills and knowledge throughout your life.

Critical thinking and problem-solving: Develop your ability to think critically and solve complex problems. These skills are essential in navigating the challenges of the future. Imagine a future where you use these abilities to innovate and create solutions that benefit society.

Collaboration and communication: Work effectively with others and communicate your ideas. The future will require collaborative efforts to address global issues. Picture a future where you lead projects, influence change, and inspire others through effective communication and teamwork.

Resilience and adaptability: The future is unpredictable, so being resilient and adaptable is crucial. Embrace change, learn from setbacks, and stay optimistic. Imagine a future where you confidently face challenges, knowing that each experience makes you stronger and more capable.

Closing reflections

The future is an open horizon, filled with opportunities and challenges that will evaluate your decisions, creativity, and determination. It is a call to action for you, the next generation, to step up and shape the world you want to live in.

Your journey to the future starts now, and it requires courage, commitment, and a relentless pursuit of knowledge and growth. Are you ready to take on this challenge and make your mark on the world?

The future is a blank canvas, and you are the artist. The trends and changes we have discussed are just the beginning. You have the energy, creativity, and determination to shape a future that is bright, inclusive, and sustainable. Embrace the opportunities ahead, stay informed, and work together to build a world that you are proud to inherit and pass on to the next generation.

> *Call to Action*
>
> Your future is in your hands. Every action you take today shapes the world of tomorrow. Get involved in your community, advocate for the causes you believe in, and never stop learning. Use your voice to speak up for those who cannot, and your skills to solve the problems you see around you.
>
> Embrace technology, celebrate diversity, and strive for sustainability. The world needs your passion, creativity, and leadership.
>
> *Thought to Ponder*
>
> As you look towards the future, ask yourself: What kind of world do I want to create? What legacy do I want to leave behind? Your choices and actions will ripple through time, affecting generations to come.
>
> Dream big, act with purpose, and never underestimate the power you must be effective. The future is not just something that happens to you—it is something you create.

"Rise to the challenge and be the change you want to see in the world.

Chapter 10
Social Justice and Advocacy

"Raise Your Voice, Change the World: Advocacy for a More Just Society!"

Social justice and advocacy are powerful concepts that can inspire and empower young people to create a more equitable and inclusive world. This chapter delves into the meaning of social justice and advocacy, explores their importance, and provides concrete examples and strategies to help youth become effective advocates for change.

Understanding social justice

Imagine a giant playground, full of fun equipment and exciting games. But what if only some kids were allowed to use the swings, while others were not allowed to play at all? That would not be very fair, would it?

Social justice is like making sure everyone gets to enjoy the playground of life. It means everyone has the same opportunities to succeed and be happy, regardless of their background, beliefs, or circumstances. It is like making sure everyone gets a fair chance to climb the monkey bars, slide down the slide, and swing high in the sky!

Social justice is ensuring that all individuals and groups in society are treated fairly and have equal access to resources and opportunities. It involves recognising and addressing inequalities based on factors such as race, gender, sexuality, socioeconomic status, and more.

Key elements of social justice

Equity: Everyone has the same access to things like education, healthcare, and opportunities to reach their goals. Recognising that different people may need different resources and support to achieve the same outcomes.

Equality: Treating everyone with respect, regardless of their differences. Ensuring everyone has the same opportunities and rights.

Inclusion: Making sure everyone feels welcome and valued and has a seat at the table. Creating environments where everyone feels welcome and valued.

Diversity: Recognising and appreciating that everyone has something unique to offer, even if they come from diverse backgrounds. Valuing and respecting differences among people.

Human Rights: Protecting the basic rights and freedoms to which all humans are entitled.

So, why is social justice important for young people like you? Because you are the future!

By learning about and working towards social justice, you can help create a world where everyone has the chance to reach their full potential and live a happy life. You can be the voice for those who might not be heard and help build a playground where everyone gets to play!

Some key issues in social justice include:

Racial inequality

Racial inequality involves systemic discrimination and unequal treatment based on race or ethnicity. This manifests in various areas such as education, employment, housing, healthcare, and the criminal justice system.

   - ***Impact:*** Communities of colour often face higher rates of poverty, limited access to quality education and healthcare.

   - ***Action:*** Addressing racial inequality requires implementing policies that promote equal opportunities, dismantling discriminatory practices, and fostering inclusive environments through education and advocacy.

Gender equality

Gender equality pertains to the equal rights, responsibilities, and opportunities of individuals regardless of their gender. Despite progress, disparities persist in areas like pay, career advancement, and representation.

- **Impact:** Women and non-binary individuals often face wage gaps, underrepresentation in leadership roles, and gender-based violence.

- **Action:** Promoting gender equality involves enacting equal pay legislation, ensuring access to reproductive healthcare, and creating safe spaces for all genders through policy changes and cultural shifts.

Economic inequality

Economic inequality refers to the unequal distribution of wealth and resources within a society. This can lead to significant disparities in living standards, education, and healthcare.

- **Impact:** Individuals from lower socioeconomic backgrounds may experience limited access to quality education, healthcare, and job opportunities, perpetuating cycles of poverty.

- **Action:** Addressing economic inequality requires progressive taxation, increasing the minimum wage, expanding access to affordable education and healthcare, and creating job opportunities through economic policies.

Healthcare access

Healthcare access involves ensuring that all individuals can obtain necessary medical services. Barriers to access can include cost, location, and discrimination.

- **Impact:** Limited access to healthcare can lead to untreated illnesses, higher mortality rates, and overall poorer health outcomes for marginalized populations.

- **Action:** Improving healthcare access involves expanding public healthcare programs, reducing costs of medical services, and ensuring non-discriminatory practices in healthcare settings.

Educational equity

Educational equity means that all students, regardless of their background, have access to high-quality education. Disparities can arise from funding differences, resource availability, and biased curricula.

- **Impact**: Inequities in education contribute to achievement gaps, lower graduation rates and limited career prospects for students from disadvantaged backgrounds.

- **Action:** Achieving educational equity requires equitable funding for schools, inclusive curricula, and support services for students facing barriers to learning.

Disability rights

Disability rights ensure that individuals with disabilities have equal opportunities and access to all aspects of life, including education, employment, and public services.

- **Impact:** People with disabilities often encounter physical, social, and systemic barriers that limit their participation in society.

- **Action:** Promoting disability rights requires enforcing accessibility standards, providing support services, and fostering inclusive attitudes through public awareness campaigns.

Environmental justice

Environmental justice addresses the fair distribution of environmental benefits and burdens, ensuring that no group bears an unequal share of negative environmental impacts.

- **Impact:** Marginalised communities often face higher exposure to pollution, limited access to clean water and air, and greater vulnerability to climate change effects.

- **Action:** Achieving environmental justice involves implementing policies that protect vulnerable communities, promoting sustainable practices, and ensuring equitable access to natural resources.

Addressing these key issues of social justice requires a multifaceted approach involving policy changes, community engagement, and sustained advocacy efforts. By working towards solutions in these areas, society can move closer to achieving equity and justice for all.

What is advocacy?

Advocacy is the act of officially supporting or recommending a particular cause, policy, or idea. Advocates work to influence decision-making within political, economic, and social systems to bring about change or raise awareness about critical issues.

Advocacy can take many forms, including lobbying government officials, organising campaigns, engaging in public education, and mobilising communities. The goal of advocacy is to promote positive change, advance social justice, and address issues affecting individuals or communities.

Advocacy is about speaking up for what you believe in and working to create positive change. It means using your voice, skills, and actions to support a cause, help others, and make the world a better place.

Youth play a crucial role in advocacy, bringing a unique perspective and powerful voice to critical issues.

Types of advocacies

Individual advocacy: Helping someone on a personal level, like supporting a friend who is being bullied.

Group advocacy: Working with others to address a common issue, such as forming a club to promote recycling at school.

Systemic advocacy: Aiming to change policies and practices at a larger scale, like campaigning for climate action laws.

The role of Youth in social justice and advocacy

Young people have always been at the forefront of social change. Here are some reasons why youth are powerful advocates:

Raising awareness

Youth play a crucial role in bringing attention to social justice issues by leveraging social media, organizing campaigns, and participating in public demonstrations.

   - **Example:** Through viral social media campaigns or organising school protests, young people can amplify their voices and highlight issues such as climate change, racial inequality, and gender discrimination.

Advocating for policy change

Youth can influence public policy by engaging in advocacy efforts, meeting with policymakers, and participating in youth Councils or Advisory Boards.

- **Example:** Lobbying for environmental regulations, supporting legislation or campaigning for educational reforms are ways youth can impact policy decisions at local, national, or global levels.

Engaging in community service

Volunteering and participating in community service projects enable youth to directly contribute to addressing social issues and supporting marginalised groups.

- **Example:** Organising food drives, mentoring at-risk youth, or participating in clean-up efforts in underserved neighbourhoods are tangible ways youth can be effective in their communities.

Promoting inclusivity and representation

Youth can advocate for greater inclusivity and representation within institutions, media, and organisations, ensuring diverse voices are heard and valued.

- **Example:** Starting or joining groups that focus on amplifying marginalized voices, such as diversity clubs or advocacy organiSations, helps to create more inclusive environments.

Educating and empowering peers

By sharing knowledge and raising awareness among their peers, youth can foster a culture of understanding and activism within their schools and communities.

- **Example:** Hosting workshops, creating educational content, or leading discussions on topics like mental health, social justice, and equality empowers others to take informed action.

Innovating solutions

Youth often bring fresh perspectives and innovative ideas to social justice issues, creating innovative solutions and approaches to longstanding problems.

- **Example:** Developing apps for social change, starting non-profit organisations, or inventing sustainable products are ways youth contribute creative solutions to social challenges.

Building alliances and networks

Forming alliances with other youth, organisations, and community leaders enhances the effectiveness of advocacy efforts and broadens the impact of social justice initiatives.

- **Example:** Collaborating on cross-cultural projects, joining international youth forums, or participating in global movements like "Fridays for Future" strengthens collective action for social justice.

Challenging inequities

Youth can actively challenge and confront systemic inequities and injustices by speaking out against discrimination, advocating for systemic reforms, and demanding accountability.

- **Example:** Engaging in campaigns to address systemic racism, gender inequality, or economic disparity encourages societal change and promotes justice.

Leading by example

Demonstrating ethical behaviour, empathy, and commitment to social justice issues sets a positive example for others and inspires collective action.

- **Example:** Youth who volunteer, engage in respectful dialogue, and live according to principles of fairness and equality motivate others to do the same.

By embracing these roles, youth can drive considerable progress in social justice and advocacy, contributing to a more equitable and inclusive society. Their energy, creativity, and passion are essential in addressing current issues and shaping a better future.

Strategies for effective advocacy

Raising awareness

Social media campaigns: Use platforms like Instagram, TikTok, or Twitter to spread awareness about issues you care about. Create engaging content, share stories, and use relevant hashtags to reach a wider audience.

Organise events: Host awareness campaigns, workshops, or information sessions in your school, community centers, or online. Invite experts or people directly impacted by the issue to share their perspectives.

Creative expression: Use art, music, poetry, or film to raise awareness and spark conversation about critical issues.

Empowering others

Peer-to-peer education: Organise workshops or discussions in your school or community to educate others about the issue and different advocacy approaches.

Mentorship programs: Become a mentor to younger students or individuals new to advocacy, sharing your knowledge and experience.

Acting

Petitions and letters: Gather signatures for online petitions or write letters to local officials, urging them to address the issue.

Peaceful protests and rallies: Organise and participate in peaceful protests or rallies to express your concerns and demands for change.

Volunteer your time: Volunteer with organisations working towards the cause you care about. This allows you to contribute directly and gain valuable experience.

Amplifying diverse voices

Support marginalised groups: Advocate for the rights and needs of marginalised groups within your community or globally. Promote inclusivity and ensure everyone's voices are heard.

Use inclusive language: Be mindful of the language you use when discussing diverse groups of people. Use respectful and inclusive terms that recognise individual experiences and avoid perpetuating stereotypes.

By bringing their unique perspectives, creative energy, and unwavering passion, young people can be powerful advocates for change and create a more just and equitable world.

The role of advocacy in promoting social justice

Advocacy plays a crucial role in promoting social justice by raising awareness about injustices, advocating for policy changes, and supporting marginalised communities. Advocates work to address systemic issues and empower individuals to create positive change.

Strategies for effective advocacy

Effective advocacy involves:

Education and awareness. Educating others about social justice issues and their impact through hosting workshops or seminars to educate others about social justice issues.

Coalition building. Building alliances with like-minded individuals and organisations.

Policy advocacy. Advocating for policy changes at the local, national, and international levels by lobbying lawmakers to pass legislation that promotes equality and justice.

Direct action. Engaging in protests, marches, and other forms of direct action to raise awareness and pressure decision-makers through organising a protest or rally to raise awareness about a specific social justice issue.

These examples illustrate how advocacy can be used as a tool to promote social justice and create positive change in society.

The impact of social justice and advocacy on society

Social justice and advocacy have profound effects on society, shaping its values, norms, and structures. Here are some key impacts:

Promoting equality. Social justice and advocacy strive to ensure that all individuals, regardless of background, have equal rights and opportunities. This promotes a more fair and inclusive society where everyone can thrive.

Addressing injustice. Advocacy efforts often target specific issues of injustice, such as discrimination, poverty, and inequality. By raising awareness and mobilising support, advocates work to address these issues and create positive change.

Empowering marginalised communities. Social justice and advocacy empower marginalised communities by amplifying their voices, advocating for their rights, and challenging oppressive systems. This can lead to greater representation and inclusion in society.

Fostering diversity and inclusion. Advocacy for social justice encourages diversity and inclusion by challenging stereotypes, promoting acceptance of diverse backgrounds and perspectives, and creating spaces where everyone feels valued and respected.

Policy changes. Advocacy efforts often lead to changes in policies and laws that promote greater social justice. These changes can have far-reaching effects, impacting entire communities or even nations.

Cultural shifts. Social justice advocacy can also lead to cultural shifts, changing societal attitudes and beliefs about critical issues. This can help reduce stigma, increase empathy, and create a more compassionate society.

Inspiring future generations. By promoting values of fairness, equality, and justice, social justice advocacy inspires future generations to continue the work of creating a better world for all.

Becoming positive change agents: The power of responsible advocacy

In today's world, young people are not just the leaders of tomorrow; they are also the voices of today. As Youth, you have the power to create meaningful change in your communities and beyond. However, advocacy comes with responsibilities. The following explores how we can be effective advocates for positive change, emphasising the importance of providing solutions rather than engaging in destructive actions.

Understanding responsible advocacy

Advocacy is about speaking up for what you believe in and working to be effective. Responsible advocacy means doing this in a way that is thoughtful, constructive, and respectful. It involves understanding the issues you care about, researching workable solutions, and engaging with others positively and inclusively.

Providing solutions, not destruction

One of the key principles of responsible advocacy is focusing on providing solutions rather than engaging in destructive behaviour. Destruction, whether physical or verbal, rarely leads to lasting change. Instead, it often creates more problems and divides communities.

As young advocates, you have the creativity and energy to produce innovative solutions to complex problems. By channelling your efforts into constructive actions, you can make a real difference.

Tips for responsible advocacy

1. Educate yourself. Take the time to learn about the issues you care about. Understand the root causes and workable solutions.

2. Be respectful. Treat others with respect, even if you disagree with them. Respectful dialogue is more likely to lead to positive outcomes.

3. Collaborate. Work with others who share your goals. Collaboration can amplify your impact and bring diverse perspectives to the table.

4. Stay positive. Maintain a cheerful outlook, even in the face of challenges. Positivity is contagious and can inspire others to join your cause.

5. Act. Put your ideas into action. Whether it is organising a community event, starting a petition, or simply raising awareness, every action counts.

As young advocates, you have the power to shape the future. By being responsible, positive changemakers, you can inspire others to join you in creating a better world for all.

Remember, advocacy is not about tearing down what is wrong, but about building up what is right. Together, we can be effective.

Closing reflections

Advocacy and social justice are powerful tools that can create profound change in our communities and the world. As youth, you possess unique perspectives, energy, and the capacity to challenge the status quo and fight for what is right. By understanding the principles of social justice, recognising the importance of equity, and learning how to effectively advocate for change, you can make a significant impact.

Remember, advocacy starts with awareness and education. Equip yourself with knowledge about the issues that matter to you and those affecting your community. Use your voice to speak up against injustice and amplify the voices of those who may not be heard. Engage in community initiatives, join or start organisations that focus on social justice, and use creative means like art, writing, and social media to spread your message.

As you move forward, keep in mind that true change is a collective effort. Build alliances, work collaboratively, and support one another in your endeavours. Together, you can create a future where everyone is treated with dignity, respect, and fairness. Your journey as an advocate for social justice is just beginning, and the possibilities for what you can achieve are endless. Embrace this role with passion, commitment, and hope, knowing that you have the power to have influence.

Call to Action

Your voice matters. Use it to stand up for what you believe in and to support those who need it. Whether it is speaking out against injustice, organising a community project, or simply educating yourself and others, every action counts.

Every action you take, no matter how small, contributes to a larger movement toward a more just and equitable world. Reflect on the change-makers who have come before you and draw inspiration from their courage and perseverance. Understand that the path to social justice is often challenging, but it is also immensely rewarding.

Thought to Ponder

As you embark on your journey of advocacy, ask yourself: What kind of world do I want to create? Your actions today will shape the future. Dream big, act with purpose, and never underestimate the power you must have to influence.

"Be bold, be persistent, and be the change you want to see in the world."

Chapter 11
Building Strong and Inclusive Communities

"Inclusive Bonds: The Foundation of Flourishing Communities"

Imagine a world where everyone feels they belong, where everyone's unique qualities are celebrated, and where no one is left out. This is the essence of an inclusive community. Building such communities is essential, not just for harmony but for a richer, more diverse experience for everyone involved.

Imagine walking into a place where you feel completely at home, where your unique qualities are celebrated, and where you see a reflection of yourself and others in the community. This is what an inclusive community strives to achieve. Inclusivity means everyone, regardless of their background or identity, is valued and respected.

In this chapter, we will explore how youth can contribute to creating inclusive communities, learn why inclusivity matters, and discover inspiring examples from around the world.

The foundation of inclusive communities

Inclusive communities are built on the principles of respect, equity, participation, and support. They are places where diversity is celebrated, and everyone has a voice. To utterly understand what it means to build an inclusive community, we must delve into these foundational elements.

Respect

Respect is about recognising the inherent worth of every individual. It involves valuing each person's contributions and acknowledging their unique experiences and perspectives. In an inclusive community, respect is shown through active listening, empathy, and considerate actions.

- **Example:** Schools can implement peer mediation programs where students are trained to resolve conflicts among their peers, fostering a culture of mutual respect and understanding.

Equity

Equity ensures that everyone has access to the same opportunities and resources. It goes beyond equality by recognising that different people have unique needs and providing the necessary support to meet those needs.

- **Example:** A community centre could offer scholarships for extracurricular activities to students from low-income families, ensuring they have the same opportunities to participate as their peers.

Participation

Participation means that everyone has a voice and a role in the community. It involves creating spaces where individuals can express their opinions and contribute to decision-making processes.

- **Example:** Establishing youth advisory councils in local governments allows young people to have a say in policies and programs that affect them, ensuring their perspectives are considered.

Support

Support is about providing the necessary resources and assistance to help individuals thrive. This can include emotional support, educational resources, and access to healthcare.

- **Example:** Schools can create mentorship programs where older students mentor younger ones, providing guidance and support to help them succeed academically and socially.

The importance of inclusive communities

Inclusive communities are vital for fostering social cohesion, reducing discrimination, and promoting overall well-being. They provide a supportive environment where everyone can thrive and contribute their best.

Social cohesion

Inclusive communities bring people together, fostering a sense of belonging and unity. When individuals feel accepted and valued, they are more likely to participate actively in their communities, strengthening social bonds.

- **Example:** Community festivals that celebrate diverse cultures can bring people together, fostering understanding and friendship among diverse groups.

Reducing discrimination

Inclusivity helps to challenge and reduce discrimination and prejudice. By promoting understanding and respect, inclusive communities create an environment where discriminatory behaviors and attitudes are less likely to thrive.

- **Example:** Anti-bullying campaigns in schools that educate students about the impact of discrimination and promote inclusivity can help create a more respectful and supportive school environment.

Promoting well-being

Inclusive communities support the well-being of their members by providing the resources and opportunities they need to thrive. This can lead to improved mental and physical health, greater academic and professional success, and overall life satisfaction.

- **Example:** Providing access to mental health services in schools and communities ensures that everyone has the support they need to maintain their well-being.

Strategies to build inclusive communities

Educate yourself and others: Understanding diverse cultures, identities, and experiences is the first step towards inclusivity. Educate yourself about the diverse groups in your community and share your knowledge with others.

This can be done through reading, attending workshops, or engaging in conversations with people from diverse backgrounds.

- **Example:** Organise cultural exchange events at school where students can share their traditions, foods, and stories. This helps build mutual respect and understanding.

To deepen your understanding, consider watching documentaries or reading books that highlight diverse cultures and experiences. Engage in discussions with friends and family about what you learn.

Challenge stereotypes and biases: Stereotypes and biases are often based on misinformation. Challenge these by questioning assumptions and standing up against discriminatory behaviour.

This requires courage and a commitment to fairness.

- **Example:** If you hear someone making a biased comment, respectfully correct them and explain why their statement is harmful. This can be done by providing information and sharing personal stories that challenge the stereotype.

Creating awareness campaigns in your school or community can also be effective. Use posters, social media, and presentations to educate others about the impact of stereotypes and biases and how to combat them.

Create inclusive spaces: Ensure that physical and social spaces are welcoming to everyone. This could mean making facilities accessible to people with disabilities or creating safe spaces where people can express themselves without fear of judgment.

-**Example:** Advocate for ramps and elevators in your school to make it accessible to everyone, including those who use wheelchairs. Also, consider creating quiet rooms for students who need a calm environment to focus or relax.

Inclusivity in spaces also means ensuring that events and activities are designed to be accessible to all. This includes providing sign language interpreters, ensuring venues are wheelchair accessible, and offering materials in multiple languages.

Encourage participation: Invite everyone to participate in community activities and decision-making processes. This ensures diverse voices are heard and valued. Participation can be encouraged through inclusive policies and practices.

- **Example:** Set up a student council that represents diverse groups within the school and works on initiatives to improve inclusivity. Ensure that meetings are scheduled at times that are convenient for everyone and that all members have an equal opportunity to speak.

Additionally, creating subcommittees focused on specific issues such as accessibility, cultural events, or anti-bullying can provide more targeted opportunities for participation and leadership.

Support and empathy

Be supportive and empathetic towards others. Understand that everyone faces different challenges, and offering a helping hand can make a significant difference. Empathy involves putting yourself in someone else's shoes and understanding their experiences and emotions.

-Example: If a classmate is struggling with language barriers, offer to help them with their assignments or involve them in group activities. This not only helps the individual but also fosters a sense of community and belonging.

Empathy can also be fostered through peer mentoring programs where older students support younger ones, or through buddy systems that pair students from diverse backgrounds to learn from each other.

Real-life examples of inclusive communities
School No. 21 in Russia

This school integrates children with disabilities into regular classes, providing necessary support and promoting mutual respect and understanding among students. The school has implemented inclusive teaching methods and provides resources such as special education teachers and accessible learning materials.

Students are encouraged to work together on projects, fostering cooperation and mutual understanding. This inclusive approach not only benefits students with disabilities but also teaches all students the value of diversity and collaboration.

Interfaith Youth Core (IFYC) in the USA

IFYC brings together young people from different religious backgrounds to collaborate on social action projects, fostering interfaith understanding and cooperation. By working together on common goals, participants learn to appreciate and respect each other's beliefs and traditions.

Projects have included building homes for those in need, organising food drives, and hosting interfaith dialogues. These activities help break down barriers and build lasting relationships based on mutual respect and shared values.

Johannesburg Student Council

South Africa is called "The Rainbow Nation" due to its diverse cultures and inclusive communities. The City of Johannesburg Council established a similar Student Council consisting of more than one hundred energetic Youth from sixty high schools. The students are from diverse geographic areas, genders, religions, and cultural backgrounds, highlighting unity and fairness. Each Councillor has an opportunity to gain experience from the diverse perspectives of their peers and contribute constructively to the mission of the Johannesburg Student Council.

It is a platform for young people to share their perspectives, concerns, and ideas. They can advise on policies, programs, and initiatives that impact Youth, ensuring that their voices are heard, and their needs are addressed.

Activities to promote inclusivity in communities

Inclusive book clubs: Start a book club that focuses on reading and discussing books by authors from diverse backgrounds. This can help broaden perspectives and promote understanding.

Art for inclusivity: Organise art projects that celebrate diversity and inclusivity. This can include murals, exhibitions, and collaborative art installations that highlight the contributions of diverse groups.

Inclusive sports teams: Create sports teams that encourage participation from everyone, regardless of their skill level or background. This can help build teamwork and mutual respect.

Storytelling workshops: Host workshops where people can share their personal stories related to identity and inclusivity. This can help build empathy and understanding within the community.

Advocacy campaigns: Develop advocacy campaigns that raise awareness about the importance of inclusivity and encourage others to act. Use social media, posters, and events to spread the message.

Further Reading

"The Colours of Us" by Karen Katz is a book that celebrates the differences and similarities that connect all people.

"The Misfits" by James Howe is a story about four friends who stand up against bullying and promote inclusivity in their school.

"Wonder" by R.J. Palacio - A novel that explores themes of kindness, acceptance, and the importance of looking beyond appearances.

"The Day You Begin" by Jacqueline Woodson" - A book that explores the feelings of being different and finding the courage to share your story.

"Same, Same but Different" by Jenny Sue Kostecki-Shaw is a story about two pen pals from diverse cultures who discover that their lives are more alike than they thought.

"We're All Wonders" by R.J. Palacio - A picture book adaptation of "Wonder" that encourages young readers to choose kindness and see the beauty in everyone.

Closing reflections

Building an inclusive community is not a one-time task but an ongoing process. It involves continuous learning, reflection, and action. Committing to inclusivity, we create environments where everyone can thrive and contribute their best. Let us take the first step together, embrace diversity, and build communities where everyone feels at home.

Building inclusive communities is a continuous journey that requires effort, empathy, and dedication. By educating ourselves, challenging stereotypes, creating inclusive spaces, encouraging participation, and supporting one another, we can make a positive impact. Remember, inclusivity starts with each one of us.

Remember, each small action towards inclusivity can create a ripple effect, leading to a more inclusive and equitable world for all.

Reflection Questions

What steps can you take to promote inclusivity in your community?

How can you educate others about the importance of inclusivity?

What challenges might you face in promoting inclusivity, and how can you overcome them?

How can you create spaces for open dialogue and understanding?

What role can you play in advocating for inclusive policies in your school or community?

> **Call to Action**
>
> Now is the time to take meaningful steps toward building inclusive communities. Start by educating yourself about diverse cultures, identities, and experiences, and actively challenge stereotypes and biases whenever you encounter them.
>
> Remember, inclusivity starts with you—your actions, no matter how small, can create a ripple effect that leads to positive change. Let us work together to build communities where everyone feels valued and included.
>
> **Thought to Ponder**
>
> "How different would our world be if every person felt seen, heard, and valued?"
>
> Reflect on this question and consider the impact of inclusivity on our daily lives. Think about how you can contribute to creating a world where everyone feels a sense of belonging. What steps can you take today to make this vision a reality?

"Together, we can create a world where everyone feels they belong and are valued for who they are."

Chapter 12

A Call to the Leaders of Tomorrow

"Inspiring Youth to Champion Diversity, Equity, Inclusion and Belonging"

Young people are not just the leaders of tomorrow; you are the leaders of today. Your energy, creativity, and fresh perspectives are essential in driving change and creating a better world.

Leadership is not about holding a title or a position; it is about making a difference, inspiring others, and acting. This chapter is a call to you, the youth, to embrace your potential and step into leadership roles in your communities. We will explore strategies to help you strive to be leaders and make a positive impact.

Understanding leadership

Leadership is the ability to guide, influence, and inspire others towards achieving a common goal. It involves vision, empathy, integrity, and the courage to take initiative. True leaders are those who listen, learn, and empower others. Here are some key qualities and elements of effective leaders:

Visionary: Leaders have a sharp vision of what they want to achieve and can communicate it effectively to others.

Empathy: Leaders understand and relate to the feelings and experiences of others.

Integrity: Leaders are honest, ethical, and committed to doing the right thing.

Courageous: Leaders are willing to take risks and stand up for what they believe in.

Empowering: Leaders inspire and motivate others to reach their full potential.

Resilient: Leaders can bounce back from setbacks and maintain their focus and determination.

Innovative: Leaders are open to innovative ideas and can think creatively to solve problems.

Collaborative: Leaders work well with others and understand the importance of teamwork.

Strategies to strive to be leaders

Effective leadership is not a trait reserved for a select few but a set of skills and qualities that can be developed through deliberate practice and engagement. Striving to be a leader involves more than just holding a title or position; it requires a commitment to personal growth, the ability to inspire and guide others, and the courage to act.

Developing leadership skills is a journey that involves understanding yourself, learning continuously, and actively seeking opportunities to apply what you have learned. By focusing on strategies that build self-awareness, foster relationships, and encourage initiative, you can pave the way to becoming an impactful leader.

Develop self-awareness

Understanding your strengths, weaknesses, values, and passions is the first step toward effective leadership. Self-awareness allows you to lead authentically and make decisions that align with your core beliefs.

- **Strategy:** Keep a journal to reflect on your experiences, thoughts, and feelings. Identify areas where you excel and areas for improvement. Seek feedback from peers, mentors, and teachers to gain a better understanding of yourself.

- **Example:** Reflect on a recent project or activity you were involved in. What did you enjoy? What challenges did you face? How did you manage them? Use these reflections to guide your future actions and decisions.

Learn continuously

Great leaders are always learning. They seek knowledge, stay curious, and are open to innovative ideas and perspectives. Learning continuously helps you adapt to change and stay informed about issues that matter.

- *Strategy:* Read books, attend workshops, take online courses, and engage in discussions on topics of interest. Stay updated on current events and trends in your community and the world.

- *Example:* Join a debate club or a discussion group where you can explore different viewpoints and learn from others. Participate in webinars and conferences on leadership and community engagement.

Build strong relationships

Leadership is about working with and through others. Building strong, positive relationships is essential for effective leadership. This involves active listening, effective communication, and collaboration.

- *Strategy:* Practice active listening by giving your full attention to the speaker and showing empathy. Develop your communication skills by expressing your ideas clearly and respectfully. Collaborate with others on projects and initiatives.

- *Example:* Volunteer for group projects or community service activities where you can work closely with others. Attend networking events to meet new people and build connections.

Take initiative

Leaders are initiative-taking and take initiative. They identify opportunities for improvement and take action to address them. Taking initiative involves being resourceful, creative, and willing to step out of your comfort zone.

- *Strategy:* Look for areas in your school or community where you can have influence. Develop a plan and take the first step towards implementing it. Do not be afraid to take risks and learn from failures.

- *Example:* If you notice a need for a recycling program at your school, take the lead in organising a team to set up recycling bins and educate students about environmental sustainability.

Serve your community

Leadership is about service. Serving your community allows you to make a positive impact and demonstrate your commitment to the well-being of others. Community service also helps you develop important skills and gain valuable experience.

- *Strategy:* Get involved in community service projects and volunteer opportunities. Identify causes you are enthusiastic about and dedicate your time and energy to supporting them.

- *Example:* Volunteer at a local food bank, participate in a community clean-up, or mentor younger students. These activities not only benefit the community but also help you develop leadership skills.

Advocate for change

Leaders advocate for positive change. They use their voice to raise awareness about critical issues and influence others to act. Advocacy involves speaking out, organising campaigns, and working towards systemic change.

- *Strategy:* Identify issues that are important to you and your community. Use social media, organise events, and collaborate with others to raise awareness and advocate for change.

- *Example:* If you are enthusiastic about mental health, organise a mental health awareness week at your school, including workshops, guest speakers, and resources for students.

Embrace diversity

Inclusive leaders value and celebrate diversity. They understand that different perspectives and experiences enrich the community and lead to better outcomes. Embracing diversity involves promoting equity and inclusion.

- *Strategy:* Educate yourself about diverse cultures, identities, and experiences. Promote inclusive practices and stand up against discrimination and biases.

- *Example:* Start a multicultural club at your school where students can share their cultures, traditions, and experiences. Organise events that celebrate diversity and promote understanding.

Practice resilience

Resilience is the ability to recover from setbacks and keep moving forward. It is an essential quality for leaders, who often face challenges and obstacles.

- *Strategy:* Develop a positive mindset and learn coping strategies to deal with stress and setbacks. Surround yourself with supportive people who encourage and uplift you.

- **Example:** When faced with a tricky situation, take a moment to reflect on what you can learn from it. Use setbacks as opportunities to gain experience and improve.

Innovate and problem solve

Leaders are often called upon to solve problems and find innovative solutions. This requires creativity, critical thinking, and the ability to see opportunities where others see challenges.

- **Strategy:** Cultivate a mindset of curiosity and creativity. Approach problems with an open mind and consider multiple solutions. Encourage brainstorming and collaboration to generate innovative ideas.

- **Example:** If your school is facing a challenge, such as a lack of extracurricular activities, propose creative solutions, like starting new clubs or organising events that cater to different interests.

Cultivate emotional intelligence

Emotional intelligence (EQ) is the ability to understand and manage your own emotions, as well as recognise and influence the emotions of others. It is a crucial skill for leaders, helping them build strong relationships and navigate social complexities.

Strategy: Practice self-awareness, self-regulation, empathy, and social skills. Reflect on your emotional responses and learn to manage them effectively.

- **Example:** During group projects, pay attention to how your peers are feeling. Use empathy to support and motivate them and address any conflicts or issues with understanding and tact.

Craft your brand

Your brand is how you present yourself to the world. It is the unique combination of your skills, experiences, and personality that make you stand out. Crafting your brand involves defining who you are, what you stand for, and how you want to be perceived.

Strategy: Identify your strengths, passions, and values. Use these to create a consistent and authentic personal brand. Share your story, skills, and accomplishments through social media, networking, and personal interactions.

Example: Create a personal website or blog where you can display your achievements, share your ideas, and connect with others who share your interests. Use platforms like LinkedIn to build your professional network.

Raise your voice

Leaders use their voices to advocate for what they believe in and inspire others to join their cause. Raising your voice involves speaking out on issues that matter to you and challenging the status quo.

- *Strategy:* Develop your public speaking and communication skills. Use social media, blogs, and public forums to share your views and advocate for change. Be confident, articulate, and respectful in your communications.

- *Example:* If you are enthusiastic about climate change, author articles or create videos to raise awareness. Participate in public speaking events, debates, or panel discussions to share your perspective and inspire others to act.

Activities to develop leadership skills

Engaging in activities designed to enhance leadership skills will provide you with practical experience and confidence, equipping you to lead effectively and make a meaningful difference in your community.

1. Leadership workshops: Attend workshops and seminars on leadership skills and community engagement.

2. Public speaking: Practice public speaking by participating in debates, presentations, and speaking engagements.

3. Project management: Lead a project or initiative that addresses a community need, from planning to execution.

4. Mentorship: Seek out mentors who can provide guidance and support as you develop your leadership skills.

5. Peer leadership: Take on leadership roles in school clubs, sports teams, or community organisations.

6. Creative problem-solving: Engage in activities like hackathons, innovation challenges, and design thinking workshops.

7. Service learning: Participate in service-learning programs that combine community service with academic learning.

8. Networking: Build a network of like-minded peers, mentors, and community leaders who can support your leadership journey.

Closing reflections

Leadership is not confined by age or experience; it is defined by action and intention. As Youth, you hold the potential to drive extraordinary change and inspire those around you. Your unique perspectives and innovative ideas are vital in shaping a future that reflects the values of empathy, integrity, and progress. Embrace the journey of leadership with a commitment to understanding yourself, advocating for justice, and fostering inclusive communities.

Remember, the most profound impacts often start with a single, courageous step. Lead with passion, challenge the status quo, and let your actions speak volumes. Your leadership can light the path for others and create ripples of positive change that extend far beyond your immediate surroundings. The world is waiting for your vision—step up, take charge, and redefine what it means to lead.

Leadership is not confined to a select few; it is a quality that each one of you can develop and demonstrate. By becoming self-aware, continuously learning, building strong relationships, taking initiative, serving your community, advocating for change, embracing diversity, practicing resilience, innovating, crafting your brand, and raising your voice, you can become an effective leader.

Remember, the world needs your unique talents and perspectives. The future is in your hands, and you have the power to shape it for the better.

Call to Action

Now is the time to step into your role as a leader. Identify one area in your community where you see an opportunity for improvement or change. Develop a plan to address this issue, rally others to support your cause, and act. Whether it is organising a community event, advocating for a social issue, or simply starting a conversation, your leadership can make a significant impact.

Embrace your potential, take the lead, and show the world the power of youth-driven change.

Thought to Ponder

Leadership is not just about making decisions or leading others; it is about creating a ripple effect of positive change. How can you use your unique voice and actions to inspire and uplift those around you?

Reflect on the ways you can contribute to your community and lead with purpose and authenticity.

"Step up, act, and be the change you wish to see."

Chapter 13: The Power of Networking

"Relationship Currency: Investing in Your Future Through Networking"

In today's interconnected world, it is not just about what you know, but who you know too. Networking – the cultivating of mutually beneficial relationships – can open doors to incredible opportunities in your personal and professional life.

This chapter explores what networking means, why it is so valuable, diverse types of networks, and most importantly, how you as a young person can become an effective networker.

What is networking?

Networking is the process of building and maintaining relationships with people for mutual benefit. It is like creating a web of connections that can support you in your personal and professional life. When you network, you meet new people, share ideas, and exchange information that can help you achieve your goals.

Networking is more than just meeting people; it is about forming genuine connections and finding ways to help each other. By networking, you can learn from others' experiences, gain new perspectives, and discover opportunities you might not have found on your own. It involves attending events, joining groups, and using social media to stay connected.

For youth, networking can be particularly powerful. It can help you find mentors, get advice on school and career choices, and even make friends who share your interests. Effective networking involves being curious, listening well, and being open to helping others, creating a supportive community where everyone can thrive.

Distinct types of networks

Networks come in many forms depending on their structure and purpose. Understanding the several types can help you better navigate and tap into their unique benefits:

- **Personal networks.** These are your closest inner circle of friends, family, neighbours, community members, etc. Leveraging this trusted support system provides emotional strength, belonging, and growth.

- **Alumni networks.** Networks formed by those who attended the same school, university, club, or organisation can be powerful for making connections, finding mentors, and exploring career paths.

- **Professional / career networks.** Perhaps the most vital in today's world are the connections made through your internships, jobs, projects, volunteering, and industry. These relationships open doors within your field.

- **Online networks.** Social media and digital platforms have enabled new forms of networking locally and globally across shared interests and identities. Platforms like LinkedIn are indispensable these days.

- **Community networks.** Engaging in local groups, non-profits, spiritual/religious organisations, or causes fosters meaningful networks bonded over shared values and impact.

Benefits of networking

Investing time in networking provides immense exponential value. Some of the key benefits include:

Access to career opportunities. An estimated 70% of jobs are never publicly advertised but filled through networking leads. Having a strong professional network can help you uncover "hidden" roles.

Advice and mentorship. Nurturing relationships with more experienced connections provides invaluable guidance, expertise, coaching, advice, and wisdom to accelerate your learning and growth.

Inside knowledge and trends. Through networking, you gain early insight into new industry developments, companies/roles to watch, emerging best practices, and other helpful information.

Elevating your brand. By networking, you increase your visibility, reputation, and credibility within your desired career path or community.

Building lasting relationships. By continually giving and adding value to your network, you naturally expand your community while developing meaningful bonds.

Expanding worldviews. Interacting with diverse people across backgrounds, you broaden your perspectives, empathy, communication skills, and overall emotional intelligence.

Becoming a networking natural

Here are some key tips for establishing yourself as an effective, empowered, and magnetic young networker:

Have a mindset of generosity. The best networkers focus on being of service and providing value first to others without expectation. Help make quality introductions, share knowledge/skills, and authentically strive to elevate your connections.

Develop your people skills. The core of networking involves being an excellent communicator and developing the ability to make people feel welcome, heard, and appreciated. Work on active listening, finding common ground, and being emotionally calibrated.

Get involved. You cannot network effectively from behind a screen or stay secluded. Get active in clubs, organisations, local happenings, industry events, and causes you care about to expand your face-to-face connections.

Deepen relationships over time. Many young people mistakenly treat networking as transactional. Always aim to add value first and nurture relationships authentically over months and years to foster trust and deeper connection.

Be yourself. Do not try to be someone you are not. Allow your unique personality, interests, and principles to shine through to attract quality connections who genuinely resonate with the real you.

Leverage online and in-person. While face-to-face networking is ideal, social media today enables powerful ways to spark new connections, share value, and stay top-of-mind to your network when done with intention.

Follow up and provide value. After meeting someone new, always be initiative-taking in following up, expressing gratitude for their time, noting any commitments made, and looking for ways to provide value. Consistency is key.

Evaluate and nurture your network. You must always reflect on who is in your closest circle, how to diversify it, and which connections need nurturing. Networks require constant tending to remain vibrant.

The more you embrace networking with an abundance of mindset, the more your web of relationships, personal support, and access to new opportunities will blossom over time. Work the skills now and soon you will find yourself among a powerful, value-creating network, primed to accelerate your personal and professional journey.

Closing reflections

Networking is more than just exchanging contact information; it is about building meaningful relationships that can open doors to opportunities, provide support, and foster mutual growth. Effective networking connects you with individuals who can offer guidance, share insights, and collaborate on initiatives that align with your goals.

It enables you to tap into diverse perspectives and resources, enhancing your ability to lead and make an impact. By cultivating a network of supportive peers, mentors, and professionals, you build a foundation that empowers you to achieve your aspirations and contribute positively to your community.

Call to Action

Take the initiative to broaden your network by reaching out to individuals who share your interests and values. Attend networking events, join professional groups, and engage in community activities where you can meet and build relationships with new people. Remember, effective networking is not just about seeking help but also about offering support and sharing your knowledge and experiences.

Start today by setting a goal to connect with at least three new people and explore how you can mutually benefit from these new relationships. Your network is a powerful tool—use it to unlock your potential and amplify your impact.

Thought to Ponder

Consider the relationships you currently have and how they influence your personal and professional growth. How can expanding your network introduce new opportunities and perspectives into your life? Reflect on the potential of connecting with others to enhance your journey and the mutual benefits that can arise from these connections.

"Network today, thrive tomorrow!"

Chapter 14
Inspiration in Action

Revolution Rising: When Young Lives Ignite Change

In a world that often underestimates the power of youth, countless young individuals are proving that age is no barrier to making a significant impact.

From pioneering social justice movements to leading groundbreaking innovations, these exceptional young people are redefining what it means to excel and act in their communities.

Their achievements highlight not only their talents and dedication but also the collective strength and potential of youth to drive positive change. By channelling their energy, creativity, and determination, these young leaders inspire others to pursue their passions, take bold actions, and contribute meaningfully to society.

Young leaders, significant impact

You might think leadership is for grown-ups, but guess what? Youth are rocking it! Here are some more inspiring leaders from around the world who have contributed meaningfully to their communities:

Greta Thunberg: Greta Thunberg, a Swedish teenager, gained global recognition for her enthusiastic activism against climate change. She initiated the "Fridays for Future" movement, where students worldwide protested to demand governmental action on environmental issues. Greta's influential speeches, including her notable address at the United Nations, garnered widespread attention, inspiring a new generation to advocate for sustainable practices.

Despite facing criticism and skepticism, Greta remains committed to her cause, highlighting the importance of individual action and collective responsibility in combating climate change. Her activism serves as a powerful reminder of the impact young voices can have on shaping a more sustainable future.

Malala Yousafzai: This Pakistani activist for female education came to prominence when she was targeted and shot by the Taliban at the age of fifteen. The assassination attempt sparked international outrage and catapulted Malala to global recognition. Undeterred by the attack, Malala continued her advocacy, becoming a symbol of resilience and courage in the fight for girls' education.

In 2014, she became the youngest-ever recipient of the Nobel Peace Prize for her efforts. Malala's story has inspired millions around the world, demonstrating the power of education and the resilience of the human spirit in the face of adversity.

Emma Gonzáles: survivor of the 2018 Stoneman Douglas High School shooting in Parkland, Florida, where seventeen students and staff members were killed. Emma emerged as a prominent activist for gun control and co-founded the advocacy group "Never Again MSD." Her impassioned speech at a gun control rally soon after the shooting went viral propelled her to the forefront of a national movement for stricter gun laws.

Emma's advocacy focuses on promoting safer schools and communities, and she continues to speak out against gun violence, using her platform to amplify the voices of survivors and advocate for change.

Kelvin Doe: Kelvin Doe, also known as DJ Focus, gained international attention for his ingenuity and creativity at a youthful age. Hailing from Sierra Leone, Kelvin taught himself electronics by scavenging scrap metal and electronic parts from trash bins. At just 13 years old, he built his radio station, which he operated from his home, using it to entertain and inform his community. Kelvin's passion for innovation led him to create his batteries, generators, and transmitters, displaying his remarkable talent and resourcefulness.

His story serves as an inspiration, highlighting the power of determination and creativity in overcoming adversity and making a positive impact on society.

Hira Mani: This Pakistani teenager is a mental health advocate who uses social media to break down stigmas surrounding mental health in her community. Hira encourages open conversations about mental well-being. Hira Mani is a popular Pakistani actress, model, and television host known for her versatile performances in various Pakistani dramas.

With her charismatic personality and acting skills, she has won the hearts of audiences across Pakistan and beyond. Hira started her career as a host and later transitioned into acting, where she quickly gained recognition for her compelling portrayals of diverse characters.

Beyond her acting talent, Hira is admired for her down-to-earth nature and relatable persona, making her a beloved figure in the Pakistani entertainment industry. She continues to captivate audiences with her performances, earning acclaim and an enthusiastic fan following.

Sejal Hati. Sejal was 15 years old when she founded "Girls Helping Girls", an international non-profit organisation connecting girls from the United States with girls from other countries.

The organisation fosters self-esteem and helps young women dialogue about critical issues, nurture cross-cultural friendships, and collaborate to create social change in their local communities. During an interview, she said,

"I created Girls Helping Girls because I wanted to reach the most marginal and most vulnerable girls and help them realise their inner voice by providing them with knowledge, the tools, the support network, and the resources necessary to make their vision for the world a reality."

Sanele Junior Xaba: He is South Africa's first international male albinism model. He is currently based in Amsterdam and is working in different countries. He is the founder of an NGO called the "Rolled Sleeves Outreach Program," which provides prescription glasses to visually impaired scholars in special needs schools, in previously disadvantaged communities of South Africa.

As an international model, he has used fashion as his platform to create awareness around his genetic condition, which, in Africa, has been known to lead to discrimination and even murder. Sanele campaigns for the rights of others struggling with the stigma that still surrounds albinism in Africa.

He has not only modelled around the world but also spoken out about the continued tokenism faced by people living with albinism.

Suriel Oduwole (Nigeria): Suriel is a Nigerian American education advocate and filmmaker. She is known for her advocacy for the education of girls in Africa, particularly in Nigeria. She has met with several African leaders to discuss the importance of education and has been recognised for her efforts globally.

Jean Hinchliffe: Jean is an Australian Youth climate activist who co-founded School Strike 4 Climate, a movement that has mobilised thousands of students across Australia to demand action on climate change. She has been a leading voice in the Youth climate movement and has spoken at numerous events and rallies.

Aretha Brown: Aretha is an Indigenous Australian activist and spoken word artist who advocates for the rights of Indigenous Youth and women. She has used her platform to raise awareness about issues such as mental health, racism, and environmental justice, particularly in Indigenous communities.

These young advocates have shown that age is not a barrier to making a positive impact in the world. Through their passion, dedication, and advocacy, they have inspired change and influenced the lives of many.

Game changers, Youth taking the lead

Across Mexico, the tenacious organisers of **#YoSoy132** harnessed social media to expose mainstream media's biases, shaking the status quo.

In Nigeria, the call for change rang out with the **#EndSARS** Youth-led movement that swept across major cities in 2020. Despite a harsh crackdown, these activists' impassioned demands to disband a rogue police unit tainted by inhumane killings resonated worldwide, finally forcing authorities to disband the unit.

South Africa's **#Fees Must Fall** student protests represented a new wave of Youth activism confronting systemic inequalities in higher education. Despite police violence, disruptive demonstrations at campuses nationwide opened society's eyes to how financial barriers affected poor Black Youth.

In America, the **Dream Defenders** were undeterred when a gunman's racist rage stole Trayvon Martin's future. Angered yet undaunted, these activists "defended the dream" through civil disobedience that changed into a potent racial justice force. From Ferguson's anguished streets after Michael Brown's murder, emerged the fiery Youth-led resistance of the Black Lives Matter movement.

In South Africa, it was the fury of the **1976 Soweto uprising** – when thousands of students revolted against apartheid's tyranny – that injected fresh oxygen into the liberation struggle. Their rallying cry of "Amandla Awethu!" became the new generation's defiant demand for freedom.

Australia's **Youth activists** carried that same flame in their quest for Indigenous rights. The Warriors of Aboriginal Resistance, led by trailblazers like Patty Mills, rallied relentlessly against injustices facing the nation's first peoples.

Across Europe, the spark was lit by audacious student groups like **Pussy Riot**, using provocative punk rock protests to denounce human rights abuses by Russia's authoritarian regime.

In Spain, **Youths of the Indignados Movement** occupied city plazas for months to decry economic injustice.

Across the African continent, **from Kenya to the Democratic Republic of Congo,** increasing connectivity empowers Youth to mobilise against injustice through dynamic online movements. With creativity, grit, and social media's democratising power, they are reshaping Africa's future by speaking truth to power in ways their elders could scarcely imagine.

From the pro-democracy rallies of **Hong Kong's Umbrella Revolution** to the Climate Strike uprisings led by Greta Thunberg's Youth Strike movement, examples of young changemakers blase across every continent.

These examples hardly scratch the surface. For every celebrated story, countless more uprisings were quieted by heavy-handed regimes intent on extinguishing Youth's flame. But those embers never die; they persist, submerged but smoldering, ready to reignite when fanned by the next generation's defiant breath.

The torch of justice has been carried by every race, creed, and code. Countless others, young and old, are making a difference every day. They did not wait for change to happen – they became the change makers.

Closing reflections

Young change-makers around the world are reshaping our communities with their courage, vision, and unwavering commitment to making a difference. These remarkable individuals have demonstrated that age is no obstacle to leadership and that profound impact often starts with a single, determined voice. Whether they are advocating for environmental sustainability, championing social justice, or innovating solutions to pressing problems, their stories serve as powerful reminders of the potential within every young person.

Their achievements illustrate that with passion, perseverance, and a clear purpose, anyone can spark meaningful change and inspire others to join the cause.

As you reflect on the impact of these young leaders, recognize that you too possess the ability to drive change and leave a lasting mark on your community. Your unique talents, perspectives, and experiences are valuable assets that can contribute to a better world. Embrace the challenges, seize the opportunities, and use your voice to have influence.

Call to Action

Commit to taking one concrete action to address a cause you are enthusiastic about. Whether it is starting a community project, advocating for a social issue, or volunteering your time, your efforts can set the wheels of change in motion.

Reach out to like-minded individuals, leverage your skills and resources, and lead with conviction. Your actions, no matter how small, can contribute to a larger movement and inspire others to follow suit.

Thought to Ponder

Consider the legacy you wish to create and the impact you want to have on your community. What steps can you take today to start your journey as a change-maker?

Reflect on the stories of those who have come before you and how their actions inspire you to take meaningful steps toward your own goals.

"Become the change-maker you are destined to be."

Chapter 15
Together we Rise

"You Belong in the Rainbow, a World of Radical Inclusion"

Look around you – regardless of what communities or places you find yourself in, you are surrounded by immense diversity in cultures, identities, perspectives, abilities, and lived experiences. This rich pluralism of our shared human family is a source of profound beauty when embraced fully.

However, far too often throughout history, our societies have been marred by the exclusion, discrimination, oppression, and denial of basic human dignity towards those seen as "different."

But you, today's generation of young people, have the power to help finally realise the dream of creating a radically inclusive world that celebrates diversity in all it is amazing forms.

A world where every person's unique identity, voices, and gifts are uplifted rather than diminished. Where we transcend superficial differences to revel in our common hopes, struggles, and universal humanity underneath.

This concluding chapter issues a call for you all to become the catalysts of this new era of belonging for all.

As you move forward in your lives, armed with the knowledge and perspectives gained from this book, remember that creating a more just, equitable and inclusive world requires constant effort and vigilance. The journey towards social justice is not an easy one, but it is among the most important callings we can devote ourselves to.

You now understand the importance of diversity, of seeking out and valuing different voices, backgrounds and identities. Inclusion means proactively creating spaces where everyone feels welcomed, respected and able to fully participate. Equity involves analysing and restructuring systems to identify and dismantle barriers that have unfairly disadvantaged groups over others.

Cultivating a true sense of belonging – where we appreciate our similarities while celebrating our uniquities – is crucial for any community to thrive. As emerging leaders, you must champion these ideals, hold institutions, and power structures accountable to them. Network widely, build allyship across all divides, and lift others as you climb.

The world is increasingly globalised and interconnected. Your actions create ripples that extend far beyond your local circles. Embracing a global perspective and seeking inspiration from diverse cultures and contexts can expand your thinking in transformative ways.

Though the road is long, and obstacles are certain, a new generation of changemakers can reshape society. You have a powerful voice – use it wisely and use it loudly to create lasting positive change.

The future is unwritten; through courage, compassion and sustained effort, you can build a reality that embraces social justice, equity and human dignity for all people, everywhere. The work starts today and continues for a lifetime ahead. What kind of world will you help create?

For diversity and its myriad expressions, to be truly empowered, society must uplift historically marginalised identities, narratives, traditions, and ways of being as equally valid, visible, beautiful, and interwoven into the human experience. From media and education to daily practices, diverse peoples' stories, art, language, knowledge, and heritage must be focused and made to feel cherished versus exotic or deviant.

In essence, we must dismantle the artificial hierarchies benefitting certain identities over others and cultivate unified pride in our vibrant pluralism. This radically inclusive vision sees diversity not as something to merely "tolerate," but as a conscious ethic that fundamentally enriches our lives, communities, and human understanding through mutual learning, interconnection, and wisdom.

Transforming the status quo towards this audacious reality of belonging for all people will be an immense, multi-generational journey involving every individual and institution. But today's Youth have a once-in-an-era opportunity to help catalyse this revolution.

Thanks to greater interconnectivity, some of you navigate transcultural and intersecting identities from birth. You see fluid and multidimensional selfhoods as innate and desirable. Young peacemakers unencumbered by histories of conflict are building personal bonds across dividing lines.

Your digital nativism exposes you to the world's vast human tapestry daily. Most importantly, many of your generation grasp at an intuitive level that true inclusion and equity for all people is an ethical and existential imperative for humanity's shared thriving.

To be the belonging revolutionaries, stay curious to deeply understand all people's stories and identities. Question norms, authority, and discrimination without judging. Push for policy reforms and inclusive representation across organisations and decision-making bodies.

Harness your innate idealism, fresh thinking, and creativity to spark new cultural narratives and innovations uplifting every form of diversity. Forge solidarity across causes to amplify historically marginalised voices into a unified moral force for change.

Above all, never accept injustice or exclusion as permanent – persistent courage, empathy, and our universal human dignity demand better. By nurturing cultures of authentic belonging that unleash people's fullest talents and realise our transcendent oneness, there are no barriers your generation cannot overcome.

True belonging is the destination where all our human potential and societal dreams for peace, liberation, and creative brilliance can finally be manifested. The world awaits your vision – now go forth and build the radically inclusive future we all deserve!

So, you have reached the end of this journey through Diversity, Equity, Inclusion, and Belonging (DEIB). Maybe you learned some things that surprised you, or maybe you felt your unique spark ignite. That is the beauty of DEIB – it is about celebrating what makes us different and creating a world where everyone feels like they fit in.

Think back to the beginning of this book. Remember the kaleidoscope, with it is vibrant pieces creating stunning patterns? That is still the best way to picture DEIB. You, my friend, are a piece in that kaleidoscope, with your unique colours, experiences, and perspectives. And guess what? The world needs your piece!

Here is the thing: building a truly inclusive world is an ongoing adventure. It is not about waiting for someone else to make a change – it is about each of us acting, big or small.

This is not the end of the story; it is just the beginning of your own DEIB adventure. So, unleash your inner rainbow, embrace your unique colours, and keep shining bright! The world needs your light.

Call to Action

Commit to taking decisive action today to harness your potential and effect change. Identify a cause or issue you are enthusiastic about and develop a plan to advocate for it. Reach out to mentors and peers to build your network and seek guidance. Embrace diversity and inclusion in your efforts and consider how global perspectives can inform your actions.

Use your voice to raise awareness and mobilise support. Your leadership journey begins with a single step—take that step now, and let your actions pave the way for a better, more inclusive future.

Thought to Ponder

Reflect on how you can integrate your voice, curiosity, and community awareness with networking, diversity, and global perspectives to enhance your impact. How can you leverage these elements to address local and global challenges effectively? Consider how your unique contributions can drive meaningful change and inspire others to join you in your efforts.

"A single thread is fragile, but when woven together, we create an unbreakable tapestry."

RESOURCES

https://parentandteen.com/positive-peer-pressure/

https://www.dorchesterhabitat.org/the-impact-of-Youth-in-community-development/

https://www.undp.org/stories/five-ways-young-people-are-contributing-their-communities.

https://raisingchildren.net.au/teens/behaviour/peers-friends-trends/peer-influence

https://www.usip.org/publications/2023/01/Youth-activism-balancing-risk-and-reward

https://www.ukYouth.org/2020/11/Youth-workers-supporting-young-people-to-lead-change-in-their-communities/

https://www.edge.co.uk/news-and-events/blogs/marginalised-Youth-voice-must-help-us-shape-solutions-to-Youth-unemployment/

How Culture, Diversity, and Prior Experiences Can Influence Positive Youth Development - Youth.gov

Centre for Multicultural Education. (n.d). University of Washington. Retrieved from http://education.washington.edu/cme/culturallyresponsiveteaching.htm

Oregon.gov (n.d) "Definitions of Diversity and Cultural Competence." Office of Equity and Inclusion. Retrieved from http://www.oregon.gov/oha/oei/diversity/pages/definitions.aspx

Understanding Culture and Diversity in Building Communities: comunityhealth.ku.edu

Baking a New Cake: How to Succeed at Employment Equity. Human, L., Bluen, S., and Davies. R Publisher: Knowledge Resources, Randburg, 1999.

"You Can Be a Beneficiary of Racism—Even If You Are Not Racist!" Esra Klein, VOX http://www.vox.com/2014/5/23/5743056/you-can-be-a-beneficiary-of-racism-even-if-youre-not-a-racist.

Black Lives Matter: Race, Resistance, and Populist Protest Black Lives Matter Syllabus http://www.blacklivesmattersyllabus.com/frankleonrobertsr/

Showing Up For Racial Justice

http://www.showingupforracialjustice.org/

Meet the Author

Juliana Makapan is a seasoned consultant and a passionate advocate for youth and entrepreneurial empowerment. With a Master of Business Administration (MBA) (De Montfort University) and over two decades of experience in leadership development, business strategy, Governance, HR and coaching, amongst others. Her journey began with a fervent desire to make a difference in the lives of young people. A passion she carried through her roles as a devoted mother and loving grandmother. Her home was always open, not just to her children, but to their friends and peers seeking guidance and support.

Upon becoming a grandmother, Juliana found renewed purpose in advocating for the younger generation's voices to be heard. She dedicated herself to volunteering with youth organisations, where she spearheaded initiatives aimed at promoting education, leadership, and community involvement among young people.

Rising Voices is a reminder that passion knows no bounds and that each generation has the power to uplift and empower the next, ensuring a brighter future for all.

www.ingramcontent.com/pod-product-compliance
Lightning Source LLC
Chambersburg PA
CBHW072338300426
44109CB00042B/1669